LATE ISRAELITE PROPHECY

SOCIETY OF BIBILICAL LITERATURE
MONOGRAPH SERIES

edited by

Leander E. Keck

Associate Editor

James L. Crenshaw

Number 23

LATE ISRAELITE PROPHECY:
Studies in Deutero-Prophetic
Literature and in Chronicles
by
David L. Petersen

SCHOLARS PRESS
Missoula, Montana

LATE ISRAELITE PROPHECY:
Studies in Deutero-Prophetic Literature and in Chronicles

by
David L. Petersen

Published by
SCHOLARS PRESS
for
The Society of Biblical Literature

Distributed by

SCHOLARS PRESS
Missoula, Montana 59806

LATE ISRAELITE PROPHECY:
Studies in Deutero-Prophetic
Literature and in Chronicles

by

David L. Petersen

Library of Congress Cataloging in Publication Data

Petersen, David L
    Late Israelite prophecy.

    (Monograph series—Society of Biblical Literature ; no. 23)
    Based on the author's thesis, Yale, 1972.
    Includes bibliographical references.
    1. Bible. O.T. Prophets—Criticism, interpretation, etc. 2. Bible. O.T.
Chronicles—Criticism, interpretation, etc. I. Title. II. Series: Society of
Biblical Literature. Monograph series ; no. 23.
BS1505.2.P47   1976   224'.06   76-26014
ISBN 0-89130-076-7

Printed in the United States of America

Edwards Brothers, Inc.
Ann Arbor, Michigan 48104

Preface

This study is based upon a 1972 Yale Ph.D. dissertation from which it differs in both detail and theory. Several chapters of that earlier work have been excised for the sake of both economy and coherence.

I am indebted to the University of Illinois for providing clerical and financial assistance, particularly Faculty Summer Fellowships in 1973 and 1974. Thanks are also due to W. R. Schoedel for wise prodding, B. S. Childs for helpful criticism, Charlann Winking for careful manuscript preparation, and especially to S. Dean McBride for valuable assistance at numerous stages of this work. To the editors of the SBL Monograph, Leander Keck and James Crenshaw, I am also grateful for guidance.

September 1975
Urbana, Illinois

Table of Contents

Chapter I

Introduction

The study of Israelite prophecy has always been an important component of Old Testament scholarship and of ancient intellectual history. Amos, Isaiah, Jeremiah, and Ezekiel have provoked comparisons with the ancient Greeks and the Sages of the East. These prophets were Israel's claim to a place in Jasper's axial age, a period of a few centuries in which a basic transformation of man's self-understanding took place.[1] And yet many explanations and theories have developed about Israel's prophets in contrast with attempts to understand the other formative figures of this axial age. We know Plato to have been a peripatetic philosopher and Gautama Buddha, a mendicant sage; but the prophets have been labelled everything from unbalanced mantics to sober prophets of doom.

One of the most puzzling features of Israelite prophecy is what numerous scholars have designated late Israelite prophecy, things prophetic after the defeat of Judah in 587. Late Israelite prophecy is one of the least understood and yet oft-mentioned topics of Hebrew Bible scholarship of the exilic and post-exilic periods. In addressing this topic, my purpose is, quite simply, to describe the complex phenomenon of late Israelite prophecy. To accomplish this goal, I shall present briefly a theory about the locus of classical Israelite prophecy in an attempt to distinguish between classical and late prophecy, and then I shall proceed to study two major blocks of material which help clarify the "prophetic" in exilic and post-exilic Israel, viz. the deutero-prophetic collections and Chronicles.

To pick up the history of Israelite prophecy in the sixth century may seem somewhat presumptuous, the more so since I must propose a working hypothesis about the character of earlier, classical Israelite prophecy in order to argue that it radically changed in the sixth century. Nevertheless, it is now possible to understand some of what happened to prophecy and the prophetic office when Israelite society underwent severe restructuring after the defeat by the Neo-Babylonian empire. Hence beginning with the end of Israelite prophecy is justifiable.

i

First, then, what was classical Israelite prophecy? I do not intend to review here what various Old Testament scholars have thought to be prophecy's essential characteristics, since Robinson and Fohrer have surveyed much of the important scholarship during this century. [2] In their essays and in other studies, we find numerous models purporting to explain Israelite prophecy. The prophet is held to be an intensely religious man (Hölscher, Guillaume), a cultic official (Johnson), a social reformer (Weber), a covenant mediator (Kraus, Muilenburg), a messenger (Westermann, Ross), a traditionist (Rohland, Porteous), a man of prophetic consciousness (Buber). The list could go on indefinitely since no single model has adequately encapsulated the variety represented by Israel's classical prophets.

Even though the essential character of classical prophecy continues to be mooted, some students of prophetic traditions have pointed to several unifying factors. Perhaps the most important contribution of recent scholarship on prophecy has been the attempt to identify the context within Israelite society for prophetic activity. This search for a locus or social setting has been made from a number of different perspectives: Weberian analysis, form criticism, and theories about cult prophecy. In attempting to understand prophets by means of identifying a locus in society, such theories are a valuable corrective to other attempts which define prophecy by concentrating on the psychological or intellectual characteristics of the individual prophet, e.g. the analysis of Lindblom. [3] The search for a locus of prophecy in Israelite society may be more productive than a search for one religio-historical model or a search for the essential meaning of prophecy in general. [4]

A recent observation by Frank Cross provides an important insight into the social setting of classical Israelite prophecy. He notes:

> The intimate relationships between the office of king and the office of prophet have not been sufficiently stressed in the past. Of course, it is commonly recognized that prophecy *sensu stricto* emerged as an office with the rise of kingship. The standard oracle types—royal oracles, war oracles, oracles of legal judgment against king and people—were political as well as religious functions of Israelite prophecy. [5]

More recently, Cross has tied this observation to specific individuals in Israelite history. As for beginnings, prophecy in its classical form arose with Samuel in the eleventh century. And the end of prophecy may be seen in the early sixth century: "the transformation of classical prophecy into proto-apocalyptic takes place in the oracles of Ezekiel before one's eyes, coinciding with the fall of the house of David."[6] It is striking that what we call Israelite prophecy began only with the monarchy and ended about the time that Israel ceased to be a nation. This correlation between monarchy and prophecy is not accidental, but constitutes the critical clue to the locus of classical Israelite prophecy, its connection with the political institution of monarchy.

Similarly, in an unpublished Union Seminary dissertation, Stephen

Szikszai has argued that there was an integral connection between the prophet and king in early Israel. That Samuel, Nathan, and Gad were in some way royal advisors and royal anointers is clear. As Szikszai says: "The prophet's original role in the court was very likely to continue the line started by Samuel, i.e. to counsel the king, the theocratic representative about the will of Yahweh."[7] Though I can not accept Szikszai's theory about the prophetic and royal offices as bifurcations of the judge's role, Szikszai too has observed the close relationship between prophet and king in the earliest period of the monarchy.

There are strong indications that the locus of classical Israelite prophecy was the institution of monarchy. The number of prophets who are pictured as involved with the accession and investiture of the king is striking: Samuel, Nathan, Elijah, Elisha, and Ahijah. The figure of Ahijah, as described by the Deuteronomist, is particularly informative since he proclaimed the political division between Judah and Israel to Jeroboam and then gave him his royal commission (1 Kgs 11:26-40). Amos, when he inveighs against the Northern Kingdom, does so at the king's sanctuary (Amos 7:13).

More generally the close relation between Isaiah's ministry and the reigns of Ahaz and Hezekiah show a concern with the royal house. Furthermore, Ezekiel and Jeremiah consistently align themselves respectively with Jehoiachin and Zedekiah and with the post 597 communities of which these Davidides were at least titular leaders.[8] Finally, the oracles against the nations, which occur in virtually all the major prophetic books, are difficult to explain unless the prophet was integrally related to the foreign policy center of his society, the royal court.[9] Cross has argued convincingly that the oracles of Amos 1-2 against the nations reflect a knowledge of the Davidic covenant and of the identities of the participating vassal states.[10] One may infer that the oracles against the nations in Isaiah, Jeremiah, and Ezekiel presuppose a similar background. It seems reasonable to conclude, therefore, that the constitutive activity, the locus of Israelite prophecy, is to be identified with monarchic institutions of ancient Israel.

Recent discussions of ancient Near Eastern prophetic activity suggest that the locus I propose for Israelite prophecy is consistent with the Near Eastern cultural context. The studies of Dossin and Moran on Mari prophecy, for example, demonstrate the concern of these prophets for royalty. Moran, in discussing the texts in *ARM X* says: "Here only four texts have any manifest interest other than the person of the king, either his personal safety, the threat of insurrection or—this most frequently—his military successes."[11]

On the other side of the Syro-Palestinian cultural bridge, Baltzer has argued analogically that the office of the Egyptian vizier closely approximates that of the Israelite prophet. The vizier was a royal advisor, responsible for establishing the facts, deciding the sentence, and discussing the sentence's legal precedent.[12] Baltzer goes on to suggest that in Israel the prophet was a vizier for Yahweh, the divine king. Though little evidence exists to suggest that the office of the Egyptian vizier influenced Israelite prophecy, the function of the vizier illumines a similar functionary in Israel, the prophet.

Ross has suggested that the larger political-religious context for the Israelite prophet from the eleventh to the sixth centuries was the divine council.[13] The prophets served as messengers for and sometimes participants in the divine council. Most often they were messengers from Yahweh to some earthly functionary.[14] As agents for the council, the prophets consistently function within a political-religious context.

The prophet as messenger of the divine king and his divine council had direct analogues in the polity of ancient Near Eastern governments.[15] Israel has such officials, e.g. the narrative depicting Ḥanun's serious offense to David by insulting his servant-ambassadors (2 Sam 10:1-5). There is, further, evidence of such officials in Mesopotamia. Holladay summarizes the role of the Neo-Assyrian messenger:

> The messenger was an official representative of the sender himself. The royal messenger stood in the court of the Great King, participated in the deliberative processes of the court, received the declaration of the king's wishes from the king's own mouth, and then carried the tablet or sealed roll of papyrus to its destination—in the case of imperial state administration, to the court of the vassal king. Here, received in the manner befitting a representative of the Great King, he would break the seals, hold up the letter, and proclaim, "To PN$_1$, thus (says) PN$_2$: I am well, may your heart be at peace. Now concerning the matter of . . ."[16]

Holladay goes on to argue that such a messenger was the model for the pre-writing prophets. For the writing or classical prophets, he contends, a new model, the Assyrian imperial messenger, was normative.[17] These messengers, and also the prophets, spoke to entire population groups instead of addressing just the king and his officials; the speech of the Rabshakeh is a parade example (2 Kings 18). Holladay understands this change in audience and in tactic to be a significant revision in the prophetic office, and indeed it was. Nevertheless, the locus of classical prophecy remained in its original political-religious context. Prophets still delivered messages to kings, as the activity of Jeremiah and Ezekiel clearly shows, and the prophets continue to address themselves to domestic issues as well as to problems in international relations. With the classical prophets, the prophetic office and audience had enlarged rather than shifted entirely.

Identifying the political-religious locus of the Israelite prophet constitutes a valuable way of characterizing classical Israelite prophecy. Within this locus the prophet had a dual role: as messenger for Yahweh and the divine council, and as messenger for the earthly king. The ancient Near Eastern world recognized no inconsistency in these complementary functions since the king and the gods participated in the same governing economy.[18] The prophet mediated the two governing hierarchies. He could bear messages from either of the royal figures, Yahweh or the earthly king. The prophet participated in the divine council and in the more mundane earthly deliberation; or as Wright put it, "The prophet was an official of the divine government of Israel. . . ."[19] This political-religious locus of the prophet as mediator is the programmatic description I propose to characterize Israelite prophecy.

ii

Just as Holladay identified a significant revision of prophetic function in the eighth century, so I want to point to an even more momentous change in the sixth century, the cessation of classical Israelite prophecy. Though very few scholars agree about what signifies the end of classical Israelite prophecy, it is clear that after some point no one uttered oracles or wrote tracts in the way Isaiah or Jeremiah had; or at least, the canonical process did not admit or accept such "prophetic" efforts. Hence the issue of what constitutes the end of the prophetic enterprise is an issue of critical importance to the discussion of late Israelite prophecy.

Theories to explain the demise of prophecy abound and such theories necessarily depend upon a model of what classical Israelite prophecy was. Those who argue that the spirit of prophecy flickered out, think that this spirit was the constitutive element of Israelite prophecy. Similarly, Pfeiffer suggests that the authority of the law, or written word, beginning in the time of Josiah, supplanted the need for prophetic words, an outmoded form of authority.[20] Von Rad proposes another explanation based on his premise that prophets always acted within large historical contexts. Since, in the Persian and Hellenistic periods, world events passed Israel by, von Rad contends, no context existed for prophetic activity.[21] Johnson represents yet another view in arguing that the problem of false prophecy and the consequent distrust of the prophetic enterprise were the issues which brought prophecy down.[22] Similarly, Crenshaw contends that the ultimate failure of the prophetic enterprise depended upon a fatal flaw: ". . . the essential weakness of prophecy was its lack of any means of validating a message claimed to be of divine origin."[23] Suffice it to say, the many attempts to explain the demise of, or radical change in, Israelite prophecy demonstrate the centrality of the issue.

Hammershaimb, among others, has proposed a different way of looking at the change which Israelite prophecy underwent:

> In considering what factors caused or contributed to the change in prophecy during the Exile and the period immediately following, with an almost complete disappearance of the pre-exilic prophecy of doom in its characteristic form, I believe it is of decisive importance to stress the change in the structure of Israelite society which was already far advanced in the time of the later monarchy and was further hastened by the exile.[24]

Though I share neither his emphasis on the shift from doom to hope in later oracles nor his denial of the importance of kingship for the change in prophecy, Hammershaimb's emphasis on changes in society is an important insight in the search for the reasons to explain the demise of classical prophecy.

One must ask at what point the prophet as mediator between Yahweh and the royal community and its institutions no longer functioned in Israel. And it is in the sixth century that we discover the end of classical prophetic performance. To summarize with Cross: ". . . prophecy and kingship in fact expired together." Or as Hanson says: "In the post-exilic period, the monarchy ceased and with the passing of the king, the office of prophet as vizier also passed."[25] The standard oracle types either disappeared or are radically changed by the exilic and post-exilic traditionists. This form-critical evidence suggests a change in the locus—a prophet could not perform the old functions since the monarchic context no longer existed. Concomitant with the end of Davidic kingship, with the end of Davidic pretenders to the throne after 520 B.C., and with the reworking of older speech forms, we may discern a basic revision in the self-conception of prophecy as reflected in several deutero-prophetic books: Deutero-Zechariah, Joel, and Malachi. Before that new self-image, Deutero-Isaiah and Trito-Isaiah represent a transitional stage between the classic prophetic model and the deutero-prophetic view of prophecy.[26]

Rather than speak about the end of Israelite prophecy, we should perhaps speak of the transition from classical prophecy to an organically connected but profoundly different enterprise. Plöger rightly insists that the question is not so much that of the disappearance of prophecy but is rather a submerging (*Untertauchung*): ". . . a living on under fully different circumstances and in a fully changed form in which something really new has come to exist."[27]

iii

Up to this point, I have suggested that a radical change took place in Israelite prophecy during the sixth century. To proceed, we must ask, what happened to the prophetic enterprise? To investigate this issue, I wish to contrast the political-religious locus which determined the performance of classical prophecy with the context for the "prophecy" which followed.

To press the investigation of post-exilic prophecy, we must be cognizant of the fruitful lines of investigation which have recently been developed for studying late Israelite literature. Evolving out of the traditio-historical methodology, research in exilic and post-exilic Israelite texts has moved beyond designating individual traditions to investigating theological perspectives of different groups or collections of traditions. No longer do we search for a group intent simply on preserving a tradition, but instead we look for groups which participated in the life and struggles of their times and which appropriated and revised the old as well as created new tradition complexes. The identification of theological streams and the groups responsible for them has been most informative when certain Old Testament literatures have reflected a context of conflict. Three contemporary scholars have successfully used the "theological streams" approach in studying late Israelite literature.[28]

Plöger, in *Theocracy and Eschatology,* has argued that there were two dominant groups in the post-exilic period: the eschatologists and the theocratic party. He suggests that the viewpoint of the ruling priestly group was inimical to the eschatologists who preserved the prophetic literature.[29] The groups responsible for the priestly work and the Chronicler's history understood Israel to be ruled by God.[30] This community "embodied the theocratic ideal to such an extent that there was no longer any need for eschatological expectation."[31] The eschatologists who looked for a better time as promised to the exiles by Deutero-Isaiah, on the other hand, wrote literature of which Plöger treats Isa 24-27, Deutero-Zechariah, and Joel, texts called "deutero-prophetic" in this study. According to Plöger, the views of the classical prophets contained an inherent forward-looking quality, a prophetic eschatology. This eschatology, however, lost its historical concreteness and developed into an apocalyptic view of the future. Apocalyptic eschatology represented a fundamental difference between the theocratic and the eschatological groups since the theocratic establishment had no significant eschatological expectation. I am here little concerned with describing what apocalyptic is and how it developed, the discussion of which is Plöger's overriding purpose. What is important for this monograph is the continuity Plöger establishes between the classical prophetic circles and the eschatological groups,[32] and the conflict he demonstrates between this group and the leaders of the theocracy.

A more general statement of this method of examining post-exilic texts is O. Steck's work. His essay is perhaps the best argument of the need for and character of the "theological streams" approach. It is more than tradition history. The search for parallel features in other texts, even when literary contact is not demonstrable, informs the search for the "theological stream" where such parallels could not inform the traditio-historical enterprise.[33] The "'theological-streams' approach moves 'from the textual evidence (*Textaussage*) to tradition, from the tradition to the intellectual/spiritual life, from the intellectual life to the theological stream.'" Wolff's attempts to reconstruct the thought world of Hosea and Amos are very similar to the "theological-streams" approach. The goal of such a search is an *"historisch-theologie geschichtlichen Synthese."*

As an example of this approach, Steck contrasts the penitential prayers embedded in the Chronicler's history (Ezra 9; Neh 1; 9) with the viewpoint of the Chronicler's history.[34] The difference between the prayers and the Chronicler's perspective represents the same antithesis which Plöger discovered in other texts. The Chronicler's work viewed the Cyrus edict, the return from exile, and the rebuilding of city and temple as new acts of Yahweh providing a restoration of his rule. There is no room for eschatological expectation. However, the perspective is quite the opposite in the prayers. Israel has yet to be restored; the return of some of the land and the Cyrus edict are not understood to have had significant importance; there has been no unification of the twelve tribes; Persians have authority over the government; and the temple, though rebuilt, is not the focus for Israel as it was of old.

Steck, in accepting Plöger's thesis of theocratic and eschatological groups, believes that the former group derives from traditions like the Priestly thought-world and that the latter is very similar to the Deuteronomistic position. He further suggests that to describe accurately the complexity of post-exilic Israel, we must identify four streams: the priestly-theocratic, wisdom, prophetic-eschatological, and Levitical-Deuteronomistic.[35]

A final example of work in a similar vein is Paul Hanson's important *The Dawn of Apocalyptic*.[36] Hanson has made detailed examinations of Deutero-Zechariah and Trito-Isaiah using a "contextual-typological" method. In suggesting that these collections represent the movement from prophetic eschatology to apocalyptic eschatology, he places the literature in a context of conflict: the prophetic-visionary groups who had little power in the post-exilic community, and the hierocracy who controlled the post-exilic cult and political community.[37] Like Plöger, Hanson is concerned primarily with the development of apocalyptic eschatology, but he also argues for a direct continuum between classical prophecy and early apocalyptic, a conception which permeates most deutero-prophetic texts.

I should make clear at this point that I do not intend to assert there is an inherent developmental structure from the office of classical prophecy to traditions about prophecy, i.e. that prophecy developed inevitably into apocalyptic.[38] Traditions are one thing; religious-social institutions are quite another.[39] Traditions about prophecy existed prior to the demise of classical Israelite prophecy, e.g. the Deuteronomistic notion about Mosaic prophecy.[40] Furthermore, in the post-exilic period, traditions about prophecy may be found in Chronicles, outside the putative linear descendants of classical prophecy, the deutero-prophetic collections. Hence, traditions about prophecy are preserved in two radically different sorts of post-exilic literature: Chronicles and the deutero-prophetic collections. Chronicles, which describes Levitical singers as prophets, is a product of the theocratic circles, whereas the deutero-prophetic literature was produced by the eschatologists. These two literatures present different pictures of prophecy, differences which are consistent with Plöger's, Steck's and Hanson's theory of a fundamental antithesis in the post-exilic community. The texts to be studied in this monograph present traditions about prophecy developing within two basic theological streams of the post-exilic period.

The developments in prophetic traditions during the sixth century not only spelled the end of classical prophecy in the Israelite community but also established the formative pattern by means of which prophecy would be conceived in the future: the return of prophecy either in the form of an individual or as the spirit of prophecy given to the entire religious community.

[1]K. Jaspers, "The Axial Age of Human History," *Identity and Anxiety: Survival of the Person in Mass Society* (ed. M. Stein; Glencoe, Ill.: The Free Press, 1960) 597ff. My citation of Jaspers is not meant to deny the conservative or better "radical" character of Israelite prophetic oracles in which the prophets called Israel to accept the mores and ideology of old, e.g. Sinai traditions, or Yahweh as king.

[2]T. Robinson, "Neuere Propheten Forschung," *TR* 3 (1931) 15-103, and G. Fohrer, "Neuere Literatur zur alttestamentliche Prophetie," *TR* 19 (1951) 277-346; *TR* 20 (1952) 192-361; "Zehn Jahre Literatur zur alttestamentliche Prophetie," *TR* 28 (1962) 1-75, 235-297, 301-374.

[3]J. Lindblom, *Prophecy in Ancient Israel* (Philadelphia: Fortress, 1967) 1-6.

[4]J. Williams ("The Social Location of Israelite Prophecy," *JAAR* 37 [1969] 153-165) argues against the search for such a locus, criticizing P. Berger's discussion of cultic prophecy ("Charisma and Religious Innovation: the Social Location of Israelite Prophecy," *ASR* 28 [1963] 940-950). Williams would criticize any search for a social location for prophecy because ". . . in Israel's classical prophets we encounter creative experience and speech that is simultaneously iconoclastic ("Social Location," 165)." This iconoclasm makes any social or institutional location *ipso facto* impossible. I do not want to defend here the cultic prophecy thesis, but I do want to hold out for the possibility, indeed the probability, of identifying a social locus for Israelite prophecy. Williams' assertions about pre-monarchic prophecy constitute the real problem. He has not proved his assumption that the possibility of Yahweh's self-revelation at any time or place may be equated with a proto-prophetic authority, much less with a proto-prophetic office (*ibid.* 158 and 159 n. 11). This proto-prophetic office is essential to Williams' protestations against a social setting for Israel's prophets, and this office remains unproved.

[5]F. Cross, "New Directions in the Study of Apocalyptic," *Apocalypticism* (*JTC* 6; ed. R. Funk; New York: Herder & Herder, 161). Paul Hanson follows Cross in this view: "This accomplishment of the prophets is of course consonant with an aspect of the prophetic office seen most clearly in Isaiah, that in which the prophet acted as political adviser to the king and as a statesman." P. Hanson, *The Dawn of Apocalyptic. The Historical and Sociological Roots of Jewish Apocalyptic Eschatology* (Philadelphia: Fortress, 1975) 17-18.

However, Hanson's theories about the essential characteristics of the prophetic enterprise range far beyond the political locus when he offers a synthesis of a sociological approach (211-217) with an history-of-ideas schema (7-29). It is unclear how Hanson wishes to fit the Weberian thesis of prophet as one who has a call to break with and revise the established order with his acceptance of a political model for Israelite prophecy. Also troublesome is his suggestion that pre-exilic prophets and post-exilic visionaries are "carriers of the eschatological apocalyptic tradition." This presupposes a rather monolithic view of mythopoeic thought and tradition.

[6]F. Cross, *Canaanite Myth and Hebrew Epic* [CMHE] (Cambridge: Harvard University, 1973) 223 n. 15.

[7]S. Szikszai, *An Investigation of the Relationship of the King and Prophet at the Rise of the Israelite Monarchy* (Union Theological Seminary Dissertation, 1954) 230. Cf. similarly, W. F. Albright, *Samuel and the Beginnings of the Prophetic Movement.* (Cincinnati: Hebrew Union College Press, 1961). G. E. Wright, *The Old Testament and Theology.* (New York: Harper & Row, 1969) 74.

[8]D. Petersen, *Israelite Prophecy and Prophetic Traditions in the Exilic and Post-Exilic Periods* (Yale Dissertation, 1972) 24-72.

[9]A fully convincing study of these collections against the nations remains to be written. Wright's essay is suggestive for the direction in which the search must proceed, an investigation of the oracles' legal and treaty background (G. E. Wright, "The Nations in Hebrew Prophecy," *Encounter* 26 [1965] 225-237). Four recent dissertations have examined these collections. J. Hayes, *The Oracles against the Nations in the Old Testament; their Usage and Theological Importance* (Princeton, Th. D. 1964), a part of which appeared as "The Usage of the Oracles against Foreign Nations in Ancient Israel," *JBL* 87 (1968) 81-92; B. Margulis, *Studies in the*

Oracles against the Nations (Brandeis, Ph.D., 1967); D. Christensen, *Studies in the Oracles against the Nations: Transformations of the War Oracle in Old Testament Prophecy* (Harvard, Th.D. 1971); G. Jones, *An Examination of Some Leading Motifs in the Prophetic Oracles against the Nations* (Univ. of Wales, Ph.D. 1970). For a review of the first three studies, see D. Petersen, "The Oracles against the Nations: A Form-Critical Analysis," *SBL Seminar Papers,* Vol. 1 (ed. G. MacRae; Cambridge: SBL, 1975) 39-61.

[10]Wright, "The Nations," 236.

[11]W. Moran, "New Evidence from Mari on the History of Prophecy," *Bib* 50 (1969) 17. Another worthwhile essay is G. Dossin's, "Sur le prophétisme à Mari," *La Divination en Mésopotamie ancienne et dans les régions voisines* (Paris: Presses universitaires de France, 1966) 77-86. Cf. also J. Hayes, "Prophetism at Mari and Old Testament Parallels," *Trinity University Studies in Religion* 9 (1967-69) 31-41; K. Koch, "Die Briefe 'profetischen' Inhalts aus Mari. Bemerkungen zu Gattung und Sitz im Leben," *Ugarit-Forschungen* 4 (1972) 53-77; J. Ross, "Prophecy in Hamath, Israel and Mari," *HTR* 63 (1970) 1-28.

[12]K. Baltzer, "Considerations Regarding the Office and Calling of the Prophet," *HTR* 61 (1968) 574.

[13]J. Ross, "The Prophet as Yahweh's Messenger," *Israel's Prophetic Heritage* (ed. B. Anderson and W. Harrelson; London: SCM, 1962), 98-107. For a trenchant review of the problems in defining the prophets simply as messengers and their oracles as messages, see R. Wilson, "Form-Critical Investigation of the Prophetic Literature: The Present Situation," *SBL Seminar Papers,* Vol. 1. (ed. G. MacRae; Cambridge: SBL, 1973) 114-121. Cf. also R. North, "Angel Prophet or Satan Prophet" *ZAW* 82 (1970) 31-67, who attempts to fit prophet as messenger into a consistent typology of "revelation" spanning two thousand years and who, as well, argues for charisma as the essential characteristic of Israelite prophecy.

[14]The messengers of Yam to El's divine council surely represent the same phenomenon that Ross has identified. Yam's messengers speak with such authority that the gods' heads drop to their knees (CTA #2, 10ff). I am indebted to S. Dean McBride for this citation. On the divine council in Syro-Palestinian religion, see F. Cross *CMHE*, 177-190.

[15]On the interconnection between mythic types and historical-cultural manifestations of such political models, see T. Jacobsen's "Primitive Democracy in Ancient Mesopotamia," *Toward the Image of Tammuz* (ed. W. Moran; Cambridge: Harvard University, 1970) 163-170.

[16]J. Holladay, "Assyrian Statecraft and the Prophets of Israel," *HTR* 63 (1970), 31.

[17]Cross proposes the appellation "herald" to describe this functionary, *CMHE*, 189-190 n. 188.

[18]Kingship and a secure succession were gifts of the gods. For a *locus classicus* in the Akkadian texts, see "Etana" (the OB version) i, 1-14 *ANET* (ed. J. Pritchard; Princeton: Princeton Univ., 1955) 114, and for Israelite royal ideology, the oracle of Nathan (2 Sam 7:5-16).

[19]G. Wright, "The Lawsuit of God: A Form-Critical Study of Deuteronomy 32," *Israel's Prophetic Heritage,* 63 n. 68.

[20]R. Pfeiffer, "Canon of the Old Testament," *IDB* Vol. 1 (ed. G. Buttrick; New York; Abingdon, 1962) 501-506.

[21]G. von Rad, *Old Testament Theology* Vol. 2 (Edinburgh: Oliver & Boyd, 1965) 297.

[22]A. Johnson, *The Cultic Prophet in Ancient Israel* (Cardiff: University of Wales, 1962) 66ff.

[23] J. L. Crenshaw, *Prophetic Conflict: Its Effect upon Israelite Religion* (BZAW 124; Berlin: W. de Gruyter, 1971) 103. The larger issue of false prophecy, as it confronted the classical prophets, is outside the limits of this study. Important and recent literature includes Crenshaw's monograph, F. Hossfeld and I. Meyer, *Prophet gegen Prophet, Eine Analyse der alttestament-licher Texte zum Thema Wahre und Falsche Propheten* (BB 9; Freibourg: Schweizerisches Katholisches Bibelwerk, 1973) and E. Osswald, *Falsche Prophetie im Alten Testament* (Sammlung gemeinverständlicher Vorträge und Schriften aus der Theologie und Religionsgeschichte, 237; Tübingen: J.C.B. Mohr, 1962).

[24]E. Hammershaimb, *Some Aspects of Old Testament Prophecy from Isaiah to Malachi* (Copenhagen: Rosenkilde og Bagger, 1966) 109.

[25]F. Cross, "New Directions in the Study of Apocalyptic," 161; P. Hanson, *Studies in the Origins of Jewish Apocalyptic,* 9.

[26]Haggai and Zechariah I are exceptions to this rule and yet they prove an earlier thesis. These two figures are prophets conceived in the classical mode—persons working to recreate the nascent post-exilic community in the model of monarchic Israel, and in particular, attempting to achieve kingship for the Davidic Zerubbabel, a typical prophetic function (D. Petersen, *Late Israelite Prophecy,* 80-116).

[27]O. Plöger, "Prophetisches Erbe in den Sekten des frühen Judentums," *TLZ* 79 (1954) 291.

[28]In this regard, mention should also be made of Kellerman's and Rössler's studies. Kellerman succinctly presents the theses of Plöger to set the context for Nehemiah's work (U. Kellerman, *Nehemiah. Quellen, Überlieferung und Geschichte* [Berlin: Töpelmann, 1967] 182-189) whereas Rössler carries the theological streams approach for the study of apocalyptic into the Christian era (D. Rössler, *Gesetz und Geschichte. Untersuchungen zur Theologie der jüdischen Apokalyptik und der pharisäischen Orthodoxie* [Neukirchen-Vluyn: Neukirchener Verlag, 1960]).

Two other works come to mind as similar approaches, but for important reasons they fail as models. A. Bentzen suggested that a fundamental division existed throughout Israel's history, a division between religious officials and the laity. The defeat of 587 B.C. and the ensuing exile provided the context for the ascendance of the lay viewpoint. For example, Malachi represents the lay group (Mal 3:1-4) and a period in which the priests become objects of reform instead of being agents of reform ("Priesterschaft und Laien in der jüdischen Gemeinde des fünften Jahrhunderts," *AfO* 6 [1930/31] 283). Bentzen recognizes the polarities in post-exilic Israel but fails to take into account the priestly or theocratic element in the dominant post-exilic group.

A more recent study of OT literature and history bears surface resemblance to the work of Plöger, *et al,* (M. Smith, *Palestinian Parties and Politics that Shaped the Old Testament* [New York: Columbia University, 1972]). Smith has attempted to explain the development of the OT by reference to two opposing parties: a Yahweh-alone group versus syncretistic parties. One might call this a study in Yahwistic heresiology. The major problem with the book is that the parties are more complex in number and ideology than Smith suggests. Furthermore, the dominant interests in the sixth century community were not heresy versus true faith, though strife between religious parties could be expressed in these terms; rather the major issues were: who controlled the cult, which religious traditions were authoritative, and who was loyal to earlier authoritative traditions?

Many of Smith's insights are incisive, especially those into the Greco-Roman material. Yet his categories and his rationales for the categories make the resultant assessments of earlier Israelite literature difficult to appropriate. For example, I find it difficult to accept his statements about Ezekiel and Deutero-Isaiah—that both represent the Yahweh-alone party, with the implication that differences between the two are to be explained on the basis of the different proto-synagogues to which they belonged. (*Palestinian Parties,* 101-103). Surely this approach overlooks the vast traditio-historical and theological differences which separate these and other "truly Yahwistic" literatures.

[29]Plöger, "Prophetisches Erbe," 292ff.

[30]In spite of the significant differences between the Priestly writers and Chronicles' tradition-historical complexes discerned by von Rad, Plöger argues that Chronicles is a self-conscious continuation of the Priestly view of Israel (*Theocracy and Eschatology,* 37-38).

[31]Plöger, *Theocracy and Eschatology,* 39.

[32]See Cross, "New Directions," 159ff. for a similar argument.

[33]O. Steck, "Das Problem theologischer Strömungen in nachexilischer Zeit," *EvT* 28 (1968) 447-448.

[34]For the following analysis, see Steck, "Das Problem," 451-455.

[35]Steck, "Das Problem," 457 and his *Israel und das gewaltsame Geschick der Propheten* (Neukirchen-Vluyn: Neukirchener Verlag, 1967) 205.

[36]For other examples of Hanson's general approach see "Jewish Apocalypticism against its Near Eastern Environment," *RB* 78 (1971), 31-58; "Old Testament Apocalyptic Reexamined,"

Interp 25 (1971) 454-479; "Zechariah 9 and the Recapitulation of an Ancient Ritual Pattern," *JBL* 92 (1973) 37-59.

[37]Hanson demures from calling his a model which analyzes respective "parties" in post-exilic society. Rather he contends it to be a conceptual model: vision vs. reality. Nevertheless, groups formulate or use conceptions; i.e. one must speak about visionaries versus realists, or more precisely, prophetic traditionists plus dissident Levites versus the Zadokite hierocracy. The difference between Hanson and Plöger at this point is not great; see Hanson, *The Dawn of Apocalyptic,* 20-21.

[38]R. North's observations collected in "Prophecy to Apocalyptic via Zechariah," *VT Supp* 22 (Leiden: Brill, 1972) 47-72, are similar to Hanson's to the degree that he argues apocalyptic is a natural outgrowth of prophecy. Cf. H. Gese "Anfang und Ende der Apokalyptik dargestellt am Sacharjabuch," *ZTK* 70 (1973) 20-49.

[39]See the important *caveat* against the reification of tradition in M. Henry, *Prophet und Tradition. Versuch einer Problemstellung* (Berlin: Walter de Gruyter, 1969).

[40]Mention of the deuteronomistic view of prophecy requires mention of a significant movement in recent scholarly interpretation about prophecy: the prophet understood as covenant mediator. The most important statements of the thesis in English may be found in H. Kraus, *Worship in Israel* (Richmond: John Knox, 1966) 102-111; M. Newman, "The Prophetic Call of Samuel," *Israel's Prophetic Heritage* 88-97; E. Nicholson, *Deuteronomy and Tradition* (Philadelphia: Fortress, 1967) 76-79; E. Nicholson, *Preaching to the Exiles* (London: Blackwell, 1970) 45-50. Muilenberg traces this view of the prophetic office from Moses to the prophets from northern Israelite traditions: E, Samuel, Elijah, Hosea, Deuteronomy, Jeremiah, and less so, Deutero-Isaiah. He argues that the covenant mediator is to be contrasted with the conception of the prophet as member and messenger of the divine council, apparently more at home in the South (J. Muilenburg, "The Office of the Prophet in Ancient Israel," *The Bible in Modern Scholarship* (ed. J. Hyatt; New York: Abingdon, 1965) 74-97. Cf. also W. Dietrich, *Prophetie und Geschichte. Eine redaktionsgeschichtliche Untersuchung zum deuteronomistischen Geschichtswerk* (Göttingen: Vandenhoeck & Ruprecht, 1972).

I hesitate to accept the Deuteronomic legislation as descriptive of classical prophecy in a covenant-mediator, Mosaic style. Deut 13: 2-7 and 18: 9-22 are better viewed as attempts at problem solving, attempts at resolving questions of prophetic conflict rather than as statements about the way prophets functioned in the seventh century. See similarly R. E. Clements, *Prophecy and Tradition* (Oxford: Blackwell, 1975) 8-23.

Chapter II

The Deutero-Prophetic Literature

A. Deutero-Prophetic Literature: Attempts at Definition

That the Chronicler's history represents the viewpoint of the theocratic stream in post-exilic Israel should cause no great argument. Designating the literature as representing the work of the eschatologists or visionaries is not so easy a task since their writings form no coherent program like that of the Chronicler. Nevertheless during the exilic and post-exilic periods, the oracles, visions and other poetry of Israel's classical prophets were being preserved, collected and redacted by individuals, eschatologists, whom we shall designate as prophetic traditionists. By studying the literature of these traditionists, we are able to discern their interests and concerns. Fortunately, the prophetic traditionists have left us more than just organizational footprints within the prophetic canon. These tradents did more than just collect and organize; they added to the earlier prophetic words. They both preserved and responded to the pre-exilic prophetic material. These traditionists added or inserted phrases, liturgical formulae, interpretations, and sometimes whole literary compositions to the collections of Israel's classical prophets. The variation in style and length of these additions is immense, from one word (*'adōnāy*, Amos 5:16)[1] to the composition known as Deutero-Isaiah.

One issue must be addressed at this point. It is becoming increasingly clear that the prophetic books present us with an elaborate stratigraphy. Layer upon layer of interpretive accretion have made telling the compositional story exceedingly difficult. Hence, to claim that an addition is, by dint of its being an addition, a deutero-prophetic one, is to beg the question since there are other sorts of interpretive layers in the prophetic books. Willi-Plein has argued in great detail that additions to the original oracles of Amos, Hosea, and Micah derive from various intents and periods. For example, she identifies six basic styles of addition to the original Hosea material, a contention which allows her to argue with some force against Wolff's position that most secondary material in Amos and Hosea is deuteronomistic.[2] Nevertheless, to accept Willi-Plein's view is not to deny that deuteronomistic redaction of some prophetic books took place. This seems obvious in the case of Jeremiah and

13

likely in the cases of Amos and Hosea. We must therefore be willing to postulate several levels of so-called secondary material in the prophetic books. Accepting the geological model, I propose the following rough stratigraphy for pre-exilic prophetic books: original oracles/narratives, pre-exilic additions, deuteronomistic redaction, deutero-prophetic additions, and expansionistic textual traditions.[3] The goal of this study is to identify portions of the deutero-prophetic stratum, passages which provide data for assessing one theological stream of the post-exilic era.

The deutero-prophetic literature is extremely difficult to identify. To prove that a particular word, phrase, sentence or even larger composition is later than the putative date for the composition of the rest of a book and different from other later material requires a lengthy argument. Hence I offer no more than a tentative list of significant pieces of deutero-prophetic literature about which many scholars would agree. Obvious candidates include the following major compositions: Deutero-Isaiah, the Isaianic Apocalypse, Trito-Isaiah, Malachi, Joel 3-4, Zechariah 9-14, Ezekiel 38-39. These literary pieces provide the most important examples of the deutero-prophetic style and serve, with one exception, as the basis for this study. Scattered throughout the prophetic books are other shorter additions which probably belong to the deutero-prophetic stratum. One such text, Jer 23:33-40, is discussed below. An attempt to catalogue further instances would serve no purpose here.

It will be more helpful to offer a list of basic characteristics which derive from the texts which most scholars agree come from a time later than Israel's classical prophets and yet have been preserved as a part of the prophetic books which bear the names of the older prophets. I discern four such characteristics: (1) deutero-prophetic literature is to be found either appended to or inserted into the collections which are attributed to Israel's classical prophets, (2) the deutero-prophetic literature is dependent and/or composite to the degree to which it alludes to or interprets earlier prophetic (and other authoritative) words, motifs, or traditions, perhaps more concisely, it is virtually exegetical in character, (3) many of the larger literary compositions evince a general and consistent expectation for the future, an expectation which I will label the eschatological scenario, and (4) the purposes of these literatures are varied but may roughly be classified under one of three rubrics: exegetical, programmatic, or devotional.

The evidence for the first of these characteristics is organizational. Deutero-Zechariah, Deutero-Isaiah, the Isaianic Apocalypse, are all literary works which have either been inserted into or appended to earlier prophetic collections. This segment of the definition of deutero-prophetic literature would eliminate material like Jonah or Daniel from consideration since these compositions achieved authority under their own titles whereas the deutero-prophetic writings derived their authority by being added to works by established prophetic figures. I also wish to distinguish deutero-prophetic from pseudonymous literature; the convention of pseudonymity allowed apocalyptic texts to stand as independent treatises; such was not the case with the deutero-prophetic literature.

With the exception of Haggai and Zechariah, the exilic and post-exilic periods spelled the end of individually authored and titled prophetic literature. Those for whom the words of the classical prophets were authoritative did not rise up as identifiable individuals. Rather the preservers of the earlier prophetic words apparently accepted the role of traditionist and interpreter, freshly presenting the words of Yahweh to new times, but under the authority of an earlier prophet and his words. Organization, the placement of the deutero-prophetic literature, is the key to a new development in the role and authority of the prophetic words, authority which prophetic traditionists could garner for their own discrete sections.

Secondly, deutero-prophetic literature is dependent and/or composite in character. Perhaps the best example of the dependent nature of deutero-prophetic literature is Jer 23:34-40, the interpretation of which follows on pp. 27ff. Here one saying of Jeremiah has been exegetically embellished. The exegesis obviously depends entirely upon the earlier text; the interpretation could not stand apart from it. This example from Jeremiah, it must be said, is not typical of the larger deutero-prophetic texts which seem to be agglutinations of distinct literary types. Zech 12, Joel 4, Isaiah 27 are collections of elements joined by the most common of the deutero-prophetic stylistic devices, "on that day." This composite character would again distinguish the deutero-prophetic literature from Daniel or full-blown apocalyptic treatises like Revelation which are more integrated and independent texts.

An important signpost for the dependent character of this deutero-prophetic literature is the degree to which such compositions build upon earlier texts, prophetic and otherwise. The fact of such dependence has been often observed.[4] Hence let two examples suffice here for the purposes of demonstration. Grech, for one, has noted that Moab is denigrated in the Isaianic Apocalypse, (Isa 25:10-12). Since Moab was no longer a serious threat to Judah at the time in which this text was composed (probably the middle or latter part of the fifth century), Grech contends that these verses depend upon earlier oracles against Moab in the collections of the classical prophets, especially Isaiah 15-16.[5] Though the relationship between Isaiah 15-16 to the quite similar Jeremiah 48 is a vexing problem, it seems clear that "the pride of Moab" is a phrase become motif which has been appropriated by the author of the Isaianic Apocalypse from earlier texts; it could not derive from the historical conditions during which the Isaianic Apocalypse was composed.

For a second example, we follow S. Paul's treatment of Isaiah 45:12.[6] Paul convincingly argues that the Deutero-Isaianic designation of Cyrus, which is preceded by a declaration of Yahweh's creative powers, depends upon Jer

27:5-6 which presents the same sequence. And it is a dependence of both logic and phraseology. In the Jeremianic text, Yahweh, by dint of having created the world, asserts that he has the right to control what goes on there, that he wants to give temporary control to Nebuchadnezzar. The same logic holds true for the Deutero-Isaianic text. Yahweh has created what is and now Cyrus is to be put in charge. Furthermore, the language describing Yahweh's creation of the world is virtually identical in both texts: Jeremiah, $\partial \bar{a}n\bar{o}k\hat{i}$ $^c a\acute{s}\hat{i}t\hat{i}$ et-$h\bar{a}\partial\bar{a}re\d{s}$ and Deutero-Isaiah $\partial\bar{a}n\bar{o}k\hat{i}$ $^c a\acute{s}\hat{i}t\hat{i}$ $\partial ere\d{s}$. Here again, a deutero-prophetic formulation clearly depends upon an earlier, classical prophetic text, and these are not isolated examples as Paul demonstrates. This almost exegetical dependence of the deutero-prophetic authors on earlier traditions and texts results in a composite literary product.

Thirdly, though often composite in appearance, the longer deutero-prophetic texts seem to be held together by a general expectation of the future triumph of Yahweh. Certain components of this expectation consistently recur as a part of what I will term the eschatological scenario.[7] These elements provide the substance of the expectation as a sequence of events, the preparation for and bringing to fruition of Yahweh's victorious action, though the elements do not always occur in the same order in the respective texts. I am best able to present this scenario by graphic means in which the constitutive elements found in eight deutero-prophetic texts are organized according to an abstracted order of "events."

Eschatological Scenario[1]

	Isa 34-35	Ezek 38-39	Isa 24-27	Trito-Isa	Joel 3-4	Zech 9[4]	Zech 12-14	Mal 3-4
Return of Prophecy		39:29			3:12		(13:2-6)	3:1-2a 3:23-24
Theophany[2]		38:19b		63:19b 64:2a	3:3-4 4:15-16a	9:14	14:4-7	
Conflict:[3] Cosmic	34:4	38:20-23	24:1-13 27:17-23a	59:16b-19			14:3, 12-13 :15, 18-19	
Nations	34:1-3 :5 (?)	38:9-16, 23 39:1-6	25:2, 10-12		4:2-14	9:18	12:4-9 13:7-9 14:14c	
Intra-Israel			26:5-8 27:7-11	66:17	3:5		12:1-2	3:5, 13-15 :19-21
Victory and Return to Zion	35:8a, 9-10	39:21-28	27:12-13	62:10 66:20	3:5 4:16b, 20 4:1	9:16 9:11, 13	14:1-2, 14b	3:16-18
Banquet	34:6-7	39:17-20	25:6		4:13	9:15		
Restoration and Purification	35:8b	39:11-16		60:1-22 66:12-14	4:17b	9:12	14:20-21	3:2b-4
Yahweh as King	35:2c	39:7-8 :21-22	24:14-16a 24:23b 25:1-5		4:16-17a, 21	9:9-10	14:9 :16-17ab	
Fertility	34:7b 35:1-2a		27:2-6		4:18	9:17	14:8	3:10-12

Notes to the eschatological scenario:

1. Moving from left to right, these texts are presented in what I take to approximate the order of their date of composition, though such assertions must remain tentative. If Zechariah 14 and Malachi 3-4 do represent late exemplars of the scenario, we may observe the general expectation developing in two rather different ways. In Zechariah 14, the writer-compiler has chosen to emphasize the combat component by depicting vividly the destructive forces let loose by Yahweh. The redactor here is most interested in describing what will happen to those whom Yahweh will not choose or defend on his day. On the other hand, Malachi 3-4 focuses on the faithful; it admonishes them. This composition is designed to assure that those favored by the traditionists, the eschatologists, would in fact survive the day of Yahweh. Exhortation as well as the appearance of the eschatological prophet are intended to prepare the faithful for the difficult times of conflict.

2. Statements about the existence of theophanic traditions depend upon J. Jeremias, *Theophanie, Die Geschichte einer alttestamentliche Gattung* (WMANT 10; Neukirchen-Vluyn: Neukirchener Verlag, 1965) and F. Cross, *CMHE.*

3. Language derivative of covenant formulations in the ancient Near East is often used to describe the devastation wrought by the combat and is also used to describe the fertility pursuant to Yahweh's victory.[8] Curse language depicts destruction while the idiom of blessing provides the image for Yahweh's beneficence manifest in the natural order (Isa 34:8-17; Ezek 39:4-6; Joel 3:19; Isa 24:6).

4. On Zechariah 9, see P. Hanson, "Zechariah 9 and the Recapitulation of an Ancient Ritual Pattern," *JBL* 92 (1973) 37-59.[9]

A final characteristic of the deutero-prophetic literature, and here I use the term characteristic tentatively, depends upon the purposes for which the deutero-prophetic literature was composed; the literature was composed for an early apocalyptic, Yahwistic sect. The particularity of the sect's interests characterizes the literature. As we shall see in Jer 23:33-40, one obvious purpose was exegetical, a writer wished to interpret a wordplay of Jeremiah by exploring the ambiguity of the term *maśśā^ɔ*. The traditionists were in the business of interpreting earlier, authoritative prophetic words in order to make them relevant to their own time. A second purpose I would label programmatic, and here the scenario just presented is a good example. These writers were interested in ascertaining that which could be expected, i.e. precisely what could be expected on the day of Yahweh, an interest not dissimilar to that found in contemporary tracts like H. Lindsey's *The Late Great Planet Earth.* Most often the traditionists emphasized the catastrophic impact of Yahweh's victory on the earth and cosmos, especially the impact upon those toward whom Yahweh would not act with weal. By presenting a scenario, the traditionists and their community knew what to expect and could receive comfort in knowing that they, the chosen, would indicated.

Finally, certain of the deutero-prophetic texts were undoubtedly composed for devotional and/or admonitory purposes, for strengthening the life of the group of which the traditionists were a part. This devotional intent has already been suggested by Lindblom for the Isaianic Apocalypse on the basis of the hymnic poetry in this composition. [10] He theorizes that the doxologies attest to the liturgical purpose for which the collection, a cantata, must have been designed. Likewise, Malachi might have been created as a collection to prepare the traditionists and those of similar persuasion for the trials of the day of Yahweh. Both the Isaianic Apocalypse and Malachi present an interest in providing for the collective life of the prophetic traditionists. In sum, the purposes of the deutero-prophetic compositions varied, but in all three instances: exegetical, programmatic, and devotional-admonitory, the literature was written or collected for the purpose of edifying and informing the life of the traditionist group.

Contending therefore that it is legitimate to speak of deutero-prophetic texts because certain apparently late additions to prophetic collections share common traits, I shall proceed to examine this stratum from the exilic and post-exilic periods by investigating one narrowly-defined topic, the view of prophecy by the prophetic traditionists. The deutero-prophetic texts, though limited and often fragmentary, do yield a new "concept" of prophecy. The deutero-Isaianic texts present the first response to the new context of prophecy, a society living apart from the traditional loci of monarchic Israel. By examining the Isaianic writers' views of the office of the prophet we may discern a revision which the understanding of prophecy among the traditionists began to undergo. For the ensuing post-exilic period I discern four texts which represent the traditionists' reflection about the prophetic enterprise: Jer 23:33-40; Zech 13:2-6; Joel 3:1-2 and Malachi 3:23-24.

B. Revision of the Prophetic Task—The Deutero-Isaianic Corpus

1. Deutero-Isaiah

To speak of the development of sixth-century prophetic traditions and to ignore the chapters known since Duhm as Deutero-Isaiah is unthinkable, but just how to proceed to address this prophetic collection is a difficult question. [11] Rather than rehearse previous scholarly detritus I propose to treat briefly several issues in order to suggest how the concept of prophecy was shifting under the various forces created by the exilic experience.

In Deutero-Isaiah we are presented with poetry, the setting in life of which is virtually impossible to ascertain. Indeed, there has been a good bit of theorizing about Deutero-Isaiah's literature as a reflection of the exilic worshipping community. [12] Rather than mount a new search for hypothetical social location for this poetry, I propose to accept its lack of precise moorings as a primary datum for understanding this collection. The inability to define an original oracular setting for the poetry is a direct corollary of our lack of ability to say much about the poet himself. We have been able to identify historical allusions in the book, Isa 45:1-3 and Cyrus' victories, but attempts to identify material about the prophet or his understanding of the prophetic office have not been successful. This inability to speak about the author as prophet should not surprise us, since, in the exilic period, we should expect a serious revision of the classic prophetic role because the basic institutions of Israelite society had suffered serious permutation in the diaspora. Just how significant these changes in the conception of prophecy were is revealed by several texts in the Deutero-Isaianic collection.

i

C. Westermann has entitled one segment of the introduction to his commentary "The Prophet Himself," a title which suggests the possibility of finding something specific about the enigmatic author. He says: "Only once, and even then only for a moment, does he let himself be seen. This is in the prologue, in 40:6-7, which gives his call."[13] Isaiah 40:6 is the single place where the first person is said to have been used autobiographically.[14] The verse has traditionally been read, "A voice says, 'Cry'; and I said, 'What shall I cry?'" However, on the basis of IQIsa[a], "A voice says, 'Cry'; and she said, "What shall I cry?'" is a preferable translation.[15] The speaker is not the author of the poetry, not Deutero-Isaiah, but instead the prophetess or herald, Zion. This text is therefore not the call of the prophet, who is writing the book, but instead the call of a Zion figure, a personification of that portion of Israel which has been given the task of proclaiming comfort and victory.

The strongest case for taking Zion-Jerusalem to be the prophetic figure in Isa 40:6 is that 40:1-11 is a coherent unit, a call narrative describing the commission of Zion-Jerusalem as herald, a call occurring in the divine council. The text has the following structure:[16]

The Introductory Word	40:1-2
The Commission	:3-5, 6a
The Objection	:6-7
Reassurance	:8-11

This call narrative is a pattern which developed within the prophetic circles (Isaiah, Jeremiah, Ezekiel), presumably to legitimate the prophet's authority. The prologue of Isaiah 40-55 uses this old form in a new way in that it does not legitimate the poet. The passage may not be read as if it were a depiction of the author of this deutero-prophetic work. Even the classical prophetic call narratives were not intended to function as autobiography. Habel says, "The call narratives, therefore, are not primarily pieces of autobiographical information but open proclamations of the prophet's claim to be Yahweh's agents at work in Israel."[17] And without an autobiographical "I" in Isa 40:6, the book of Deutero-Isaiah is virtually devoid of an identifiable, individual author's voice as prophet.[18]

To deny that the author of Deutero-Isaiah is a classical prophet is not to deny the book's continuity with prophetic traditions. The presence of the call narrative form as does the placement of the book with its thematic precursor, Isaiah 1-39, demonstrates that Deutero-Isaiah uses the traditions of the classical prophets. Westermann has further argued, on the basis of texts like Isa 43:22-28, that Deutero-Isaiah stands in a tradition consonant with the prophets of doom.[19] The emphasis on the power of the word of the Lord, made explicit in both the prologue (Isa 40:8) and epilogue (Isa 55:10-11), is part and parcel of both an earlier and a later prophetic perspective: Jer 23:28ff.; Zech 1:4-5; Isa 59:21. Likewise the clause "Have I not told you beforehand?" emphasizes the continuity of prophetic task and message (see Jer 7:25).[20] The composition labelled Deutero-Isaiah utilizes explicit prophetic traditions without presenting us an author as classical prophet.

ii

The heavy emphasis on the Exodus tradition in Deutero-Isaiah is directly related to a lack of interest in the Davidic tradition. Deutero-Isaiah never uses the appellation *melek* for an Israelite king. For him, only Yahweh is king over Israel (Isa 41:21; 32:15; 52:7). Likewise, we have no reason to think that Deutero-Isaiah looks forward to a time of Davidic restoration. As Eissfeldt notes, ". . . for our Exilic prophet does not count the Davidic kingdom among the blessings hoped for in the coming Day of Salvation."[21] Only once does "David" appear. Even though there is a promise of renewal of the Davidic covenant (Isa 55:3), the promise is attenuated, as many have recognized. Eissfeldt's analysis of the relationship between Ps 89, a lament over the loss of the Davidic king, and Isa 55:1-5 shows clearly that the interest in the Davidic king in Deutero-Isaiah is minor. In Ps 89, the terms $^c abdî$ and *bāhîrî* refer to David, whereas in Deutero-Isaiah (44:1) $^c abdî$ and the clause *bāhartî bô* designate Israel and Jacob, all Israel in exile.[22]

As an expression of the mercy offered by Yahweh to his people, the following promise is given: "I will make with you an everlasting covenant, my steadfast, sure love for David" (Isa 55:3), a promise which harks back to the promises of Nathan (2 Sam 7:8ff.), and the themes of Ps 89. But, as many have seen, the benefits accrue not to the Davidic house but to the people of Israel.[23] There is a brief recitation of Davidic glory in Isa 55:4, but the glorification of his people provides the culmination. The election of David has been converted into election for the people of Israel; Davidic election has been democratized. We conclude that the importance of the royal house and the place of the prophet within that locus have diminished significantly in the work of Deutero-Isaiah.[24] He has reworked the Davidic royal election traditions into a promise of glory for the people. Just as Zion became herald or prophet in Isa 40, so the people here receive the glory of a former institution, kingship.

iii

The servant songs comprise a final venue in our considerations.[25] The identity of the servant remains cloudy, as was probably initially intended. This lack of precision about the servant allowed later reflection to appropriate varying emphases. Since we are interested primarily in traditions about prophecy, I wish to point to those features of the servant songs which have to do with prophecy.

That I do not beg the question in assuming certain prophetic qualities inherent to the servant figure is obvious. As Westermann says:

> This much, however, is certain: the Servant has a task imposed on him by God and it embraces the Gentiles as well as Israel. It is also certain that his function is that of proclaiming God's word, and to this extent it very closely approximates to a prophet's. . . . The Servant has a place in the history of the office of the mediator, which begins with Moses, who is also designated as servant of God. The terms used of the servant have direct links with that stage in the history of prophecy which immediately preceded Deutero-Isaiah; these are clear echoes of the complaints of Jeremiah, the last prophet before the exile.[26]

The case is even stronger than Westermann has stated. The call of the servant (in the Second Servant Song: Isa 49:1-6) follows very closely the form of the call narrative discussed earlier.[27]

The Introductory Word	49:1-2
The Commission	:3
The Objection	:4
Reassurance	:5-6

The similarity of the structural elements of the call narration to Isa 49, as well as the thematic similarity of this text, to the pre-natal calling in Jer 1:4 and the element of complaint also present in the call of Zion in Isa 40 strongly suggest that the servant is in some manner a prophetic figure.

This servant-prophet speaks to more than a national constituency: the nations (Isa 49:6; 52:15) and the coast-lands (Isa 49:6) are his audience. Instead of counseling kings or defending a Davidide, this enigmatic figure can say, "kings will shut their mouths" (Isa 52:15). He is more an emissary of Yahweh, the divine king, to various earthly rulers than a classical Israelite prophet who, though sent from the divine council, operated in the framework of monarchic institutions.

One characteristic of this servant figure requires further statement. There is a strong implication that the servant is one whose time is not yet; he is someone of the future. Many early commentators sensed this tendency and developed a full-blown Messianic interpretation of the suffering servant. More recently, proponents of the sacral kingship theory have piled up arguments attempting to show the similarity to the ritual for Babylonian kings in the New Year's festival.[28] But Muilenburg is able to emphasize this futurity without positing a specific ritual setting: ". . . the servant is a figure of the coming age . . . the servant stands at the eschaton. It is precisely in this kind of setting that all that is said concerning him and all that he has to say have meaning and relevance."[29] More than this we can not say. The eschatological scenario is not yet fully developed in Deutero-Isaiah, nor is the servant-prophet's place in that new world view fully defined. But as Muilenburg has noted, it seems clear that the servant participates in the eschatological age. The enigmatic servant figure therefore provided certain options for appropriation by later writers, certain indications of what might happen to a future prophetic figure. One of these is the basic futurity of the figure since the servant may be understood as participating in the age to come.

Because of the wrenching exilic experience, Deutero-Isaiah represents a new stage in reflection on Israelite prophecy. Zion herself participates in the divine council, and she participates as prophet. No longer is the monarchic locus for the prophetic figure of significance for the author; Davidic glory is democratized for all the people. The servant, when he is understood as prophet, is an entity of the future. These are traditions in flux, traditions which are not fully synthesized, and rightly so since the institutions described, monarchy and prophecy, had just been cut loose from their historical moorings. Only in later deutero-prophetic literature did these traditions about a collective prophecy and prophecy in the future develop into a cohesive scenario.

2. Trito-Isaiah

Trito-Isaiah represents a prophetic traditionist of the diaspora, now returned to the land, who appropriated earlier Israelite literature and traditions in constructing his message.[30]

To my mind, the most satisfactory approaches to placing Trito-Isaiah in its milieu, have been those of Westermann, and even more so, Hanson.[31] These commentators suggest that the nucleus of the book reflects the period just prior to 520. This is, of course, not to deny that there may be pre-exilic portions as well as later additions contained in the collection, but it is to say that there is a certain consistency of argument and style which may be explained by reference to the latter half of the sixth century and the concerns then current about the reestablishment of the cult in Jerusalem.[32] The author was probably entrusted with the Isaianic collections, and he may have been one of those who returned to the land prior to the arrival of the group which included Zechariah and Zerubbabel.[33]

Not surprisingly, there is little evidence of an author functioning as a classical prophet in Isaiah 56-66. There is no prophetic call narrative. Only two "first person" passages appear to reflect upon the prophetic task: Isa 61:1-3 and Isa 62:1-12.[34] Happily, most commentators agree that these texts belong to the nucleus of early or original material. In Isaiah 62:1 a voice, most probably to be interpreted as that of the author, proclaims its task:[35] "I will not keep silent . . . I will not rest," and perhaps also in vs. 6, "I have set watchmen," though here it is equally possible that Yahweh is speaking. In either case, the drive to perform on behalf of Zion is the *raison d'être* of the oracle. This compulsion so to speak resonates with earlier classical prophetic statements, e.g. Amos 3:8. The writer utilizes prophetic traditions of an earlier era.

Isa 61:1-3 is a puzzling text, though it is made up of a very consistent metric pattern.[36] Two basic options for interpreting the identity of the "I" are available. One can argue either that the servant is speaking or that the voice is the author's. Many recent commentators are content to read this as the prophetic first person.[37] I, however, favor the former possibility.

Cannon, among others, has suggested that this strophe should be read as a part of the servant songs in Deutero-Isaiah. Certain similarities in vocabulary, metric style, and theme attest to a similarity between Isa 61:1-3 and the servant songs. This thesis is further corroborated by the observation that Isa 61:1-3 does not fit well into the surrounding material, Isa 60-62. Perhaps the most interesting of Cannon's observations is that Isa 61:1-3 bears striking similarities to the first three servant songs, but not to the final one.[38] Whether this shows a line of development from Isa 42:1-7 through 61:1-3 to 52:13-53:12 must remain moot. The basic thrust of the argument—the similarity between Isa 61:1-3 and the Deutero-Isaianic servant songs—is difficult to deny, whether or not we accept Cannon's contention that Isa 60-62 cannot be distinguished from the writings of Deutero-Isaiah.

The particular elements which make up this oracle are unique. The "spirit" achieves prominence, as with Ezekiel and in opposition to so much of classical Israelite prophetic writings.[39] The use of "spirit" in Mic 3:8 and in the first servant song, Isa 42:1, is similar; in both cases the juxtaposition of spirit with justice parallels Isa 61:1ff. Anointing is most unusual. We expect anointing and the consequent bestowal of an office in a coronation ritual (2 Sam 23:1ff.) but we do not expect anointing at the investiture of a prophetic figure.

After these two authorizing signs, spirit and anointing, the rest of the oracle describes the task of the servant. The most significant feature of these descriptions is the contrast between Isa 61:1-2 and vs. 3. Isa 61:1-2 are general (the prophet shall comfort the afflicted, the broken-hearted, the captives, all who mourn) whereas in vs. 3, the focus shifts to a precise location, Zion, and more specific lament techniques (ashes, garlands and unctions).[40] Vs. 3 suggests what it is to provide comfort and how these good tidings were to be received.

One may, I think, contend that the oracle, Isa 61:1-3, represents a confluence of servant and call traditions. The task of the servant has informed the classical commission of the prophet. The "introductory word" and the "commission" penetrate the servant's task as they did with the classical call form in Isaiah 49. In Isaiah 61, the writer has composed an oracle which treats of the same arena of topics one finds in the prophetic call narrative, but he concentrates on the area we designate as the "commission." The necessity for such a concentration should be obvious: the task of the prophet after Deutero-Isaiah had radically changed. The people were now gathered back to the land. A new commission was necessary—to provide comfort for the people.

Within this perspective, it is extraordinarily difficult to be dogmatic about the relationship of the task expressed in this oracle and the self-conceived duty of the author of Trito-Isaiah, the more so since commentators like Muilenburg describe the figure of this oracle as "the eschatological prophet in a superlative degree."[41]

Concern with the word of Yahweh, another way of identifying classical prophetic concerns (e.g. Jer 1:9), is present in both Deutero- and Trito-Isaiah. The word of Yahweh is the basis for the reassurance offered in the call of Deutero-Isaiah (Isa 40:8). Likewise for Deutero-Isaiah, the word is the means for comfort, "the Lord God has given me the tongue of those who are taught, that I may know how to sustain with a word him that is weary," (Isa 50:4). Trito-Isaiah also mentions the word of the Lord (Isa 66:3, 5). But references to the word now display a new awe; one should tremble at the word of the Lord, "But this is the man to whom I will look, he that is humble and contrite in spirit, and trembles at my word" (Isa 66:2). This new awe is a definite step beyond the challenging or comforting words of earlier prophetic writers. The word is gaining fixity and authority.

One way to discern the character of this literature and its relation to things prophetic is to ask the question: how was the book composed? Elliger's arguments that the author of Trito-Isaiah stands in the tradition of Deutero-Isaiah are convincing. But the authors were different, as Zimmerli has shown.[42] The style of Trito-Isaiah has its own integrity.

We must, I think, proceed beyond the assertions about "standing in a tradition," since this is at best a figurative way of describing the place of the literature. Diethelm Michel has argued that Trito-Isaiah treated the received Isaianic material as authoritative religious literature and expounded these traditions in exegetical fashion.[43] Accordingly for Michel, Isa 62:1 is the text, with vss. 2-5 functioning as interpretation; Isa 56:1 is text, vs. 2 interpretation and vss. 3-7, situational application of the interpretation; Isa 62:6a, text, vss. 6b-7 comprise the interpretation.[44] On the basis of these examples and his other work, we may posit an exegetical activity for those preserving the Isaianic prophetic traditions. Plöger's study further buttresses this view of the collecting-editorial work which determined the post-exilic prophetic collection.[45]

The attitude toward the word of Yahweh and the indications of an exegetical enterprise in Trito-Isaiah suggest that we are now dealing with traditionists, preservers, and interpreters of authoritative traditions, rather than innovators in the use of Israel's religious past. To be sure, Israel's classical prophets were preservers and interpreters of tradition as well. But traditions and oracular collections had acquired a new authority in the post-exilic period. Likewise, the prophetic traditionists were speaking from a different locus. They had become "bookish," if we may use that term, engaging in a more consciously literary activity than that of the classical Israelite prophet. Michel expresses this change well:

> . . .Trito-Isaiah may scarcely be called a prophet. For him the tradition is apprehended in such a manner that it can only be interpreted, not reinterpreted . . . One must see that with him a new epoch dawns: the scribal (*schriftgelehrte*) exegesis which regards the tradition as a fixed, unchangeable entity.[46]

To suggest that Trito-Isaiah is primarily a reflective, literary-exegetical product is not to suggest that the book was composed in a vacuum. The concerns of the writer are much too intense to allow such an interpretation. One such evident concern is revealed by his conscious polemical tone (Isa 66:5). Hanson's study of Trito-Isaiah has sought to understand the development of this polemic and to identify the context of the dispute. In discussing various sections of the collection, Hanson argues that a development from "mild reprimand (Isa 64:7) to acrimonious attack (Isa 57:3ff) took place."[47] Basing his analysis on a contextual-typological method of prosodic investigation as well as a more general assessment of the content, Hanson traces the increasing sharpness of the presupposed controversy from Isa 60-62 and Isa 57:14-21, representing the earliest stages; followed by Isa 63:7-64:4; 58; 59; 65; and 66:1-16; up to the most argumentative section, Isa 56:9- 57:13.

The setting, according to Hanson, for these growing tensions may be found in opposing religious conceptions—the visionaries who preserved the prophetic eschatology (increasingly expressed in mythic terms) versus the more established hierocracy. Hanson sees a direct conflict between the program of restoration offered by Ezek 40-48 and that of the visionaries in Isa 60-62. In other terms, the conflict is between the Zadokites versus the visionary traditionists of the Isaianic school, which probably included some Levites as well.

Hanson's analysis—visionaries versus the hierocracy—follows much the same sociological approach as does that of Plöger—eschatological conventicles versus the theocracy. The fundamental difference comes in their dating schemas. Plöger wants to see the Isaianic Apocalypse (Isa 27) derive from the time of Ezra and Nehemiah, and the rest (Isa 24-26) from Ptolemaic times.[48] Hanson, on the other hand, suggests that Isa 34-35 come from the same period as Isa 60-62, a time immediately after that of Deutero-Isaiah and before the struggles of c. 520 B.C. On the basis of his prosodic analysis, Hanson has been able to take the confrontation theory of apocalyptic origins advocated by Plöger, apply it to Trito-Isaiah, and push the dating for this development into the sixth century.

The two Isaianic traditionists, Deutero- and Trito-Isaiah, present us with a view of prophecy in turmoil: Zion becomes a prophet, the "prophet" is given a new commission, the traditional locus of prophecy is revised in fact and in conception, and the literature itself no longer consists of the standard oracle types but instead is dependent upon earlier prophetic words and authority. Such is the transitional and sometimes confused picture presented by these early deutero-prophetic writers. For the resolution of these tendencies, we must now turn to later deutero-prophetic texts.

C. An Anti-Prophetic Polemic

i

We now move to consider four deutero-prophetic texts, two of which present a negative view of the prophetic enterprise and two of which expect something better of prophecy in the future. The first of these texts occurs as the last of several pericopae comprising the composition entitled *lannᵉbī°îm*, "concerning the prophets."[49] Jer 23:9-40 exists as a collection of poetry and prose inveighing against prophets for one reason and another. The particular text of importance for this investigation, Jer 23:33-40, is clearly a separate unit with little other than thematic connection, "prophecy," to what precedes it in the collection.[50] Traditionally the passage has been left in somewhat of a muddle with *maśśā°* rendered throughout as "burden."[51] Jer 23:34-40 yields little sense when this translation is adopted; hence I propose the following:

Jeremiah 23:34-40

33 And when one of the people, or prophet or priest asks you, saying, "What is the oracle of Yahweh?" You shall say to them, "You are[52] the burden and I will cast you off, says the Lord."

34 The prophet, the priest, or one of the people who say, "oracle of Yahweh," I will punish that man and his house.

35 Thus you may say, each man to his neighbor and each one to his brother, "What has the Lord answered? What has the Lord spoken?"

36 But "oracle of Yahweh" you shall not mention anymore because the oracle (of Yahweh) has become everyman's speech. You have perverted the words of the living God, the Lord of Hosts, your God.[53]

37 Thus you shall say to the prophet, "What has the Lord answered to you? What has the Lord spoken?"[54]

38 If you say "oracle of Yahweh,"[55] therefore thus says the Lord, "Because you have said this thing, "oracle of Yahweh," when I specifically directed you not to say "oracle of Yahweh,"

39 therefore, behold, I will forget[56] you[57] and I will abandon you and this city which I gave to you and your fathers;[58]

40 and I will set upon you an everlasting curse and perpetual shame which shall not be forgotten.

Jeremiah 23:33 presents us with a wordplay not unlike the *šāqēd/šōqēd* pun in Jer 1:11-12. Here too, Jer 23:33 is concise; the message is totally encapsulated within the play. The initial word of the pun pair serves to attract the listener's attention whereas the second member delivers the key; Yahweh is watching his word to perform it (Jer 1:12), the people are the burden (Jer 23:33, cf. also Deut 1:11).

What follows in Jer 23:34-40 is not entirely consistent with vs. 33.[59] We expect the author of the pun to have concentrated upon the message half of the wordplay, upon the people as a burden, but he has instead concentrated on the initial member of the wordplay, upon the oracle. It is as if an interpreter had expanded Jer 1:11-12 by elaborating upon the almond rod. Hence we suspect that vss. 34-40 are an interpretation later than the original wordplay, and interested in an issue other than that which the initial pun addressed. Jer 23:33 has stimulated later exposition in vss. 34-40.[60]

What does this later interpretation mean? Why has the author of vss. 34-40 used only one meaning of the original wordplay? A careful reading of the text provides an answer. In vs. 33, the context would appear to be a formal inquiry procedure (e.g. Ezek 20:1). But unlike the case in monarchic Israel, when a prophet might give a new oracle, whoever now inquires of a prophet is to be confounded by a pun. Claiming to possess new oracles from Yahweh is no longer allowed (vs. 34). A person could ask what Yahweh had spoken or answered (i.e. oracles spoken in the past) but he may no longer ask for a new word. The reason, suggests the writer in vs. 36, is that claims for prophetic authority had become so common that they could no longer be taken seriously. Therefore, the author has one objective—to prohibit the use of prophetic formulae and thereby to prohibit the prophetic enterprise as we know it from the classical prophets.[61] Use of classical formulae, formulae used to introduce or conclude oracles, was summarily proscribed. What is prohibited is not recitation of earlier prophetic words (that is clearly allowed by vs. 35); rather the use of classical formulae to legitimate new words as having prophetic authority is prohibited.

The reasons for this prohibition of prophetic oracles are probably twofold. First, the "false prophecy" problem, as depicted in the oracles and even more in the prose sections of Jeremiah, had not been resolved. No adequate test of a prophet's veracity or orthodoxy had been developed. Jer 23:36 states that prophetic oracles, i.e. claims to have an oracle, had become of little value; such oracles were simply men's own words and not those of Yahweh. Traditionally, this problem had been attacked by condemning such prophets or by proposing a verification test. Neither of these tacks was adopted by the author of Jer 23:34-40. Instead he rejected all attempts at claiming prophetic authority in the classical mode. This change in approach reflects the second reason for our texts, a significant development in the Israelite cult after the return to the land following the Babylonian captivity. Certain Levites claiming prophetic authority obtained significant status in the post-exilic cult (see pp. 64ff.). Such claims for prophetic authority were anathema to those traditionists preserving, editing, and devotionally using the words of earlier prophets. The Jeremianic wordplay, Jer 23:33, was apparently an ideal place for these traditionists to inveigh against this new "false prophecy."

To argue that Jer 23:34-40 reflects the concerns of post-exilic Israel is to raise a serious challenge to present claims about the authorship of this text.

Prevailing opinion sees these verses as part of the C material, the Jeremianic prose from the deuteronomistic circles.[62] I am not so concerned to deny the deuteronomistic provenance of this text as I am to suggest that our pericope is later than the more typical (and late monarchic or early exilic) issue of false prophecy. As I hope to demonstrate below, the treatment of "prophecy" in this text has moved beyond that of conflict between prophets of Yahweh. Rather the traditionists are polemicizing against all prophets. Thus, I suggest that the author may have been a member of the deuteronomistic school writing decades later than some of his earlier colleagues.[63] I am, therefore, unable to accept Bright's working assumption, "Our investigation must proceed from the demonstrable premise that in style and form, the prose sermons are one;"[64] the necessity of this assumption is not justifiable. Furthermore certain text and redaction-critical studies strongly suggest the contrary thesis, that the so-called deuteronomistic prose in Jeremiah is not homogeneous.[65]

Four arguments may be raised to defend the assertion that Jer 23:34-40 is not of a piece with most of the other Jeremianic prose: (1) there is a lack of characteristic Jeremianic-deuteronomistic phraseology; (2) putative deuteronomistic genres are not present in the text; (3) the solution to the problem of prophetic authority is different from the solution in Deuteronomy and in Jeremianic prose passages; (4) the use of $maśśā^{\circ}$ meaning "oracle" is characteristic of deutero-prophetic literature.

The argument depending upon consistency of idiom is not unambiguous. Scholars studying Jeremianic prose have often tabulated "characteristic" phraseology. In this instance, I refer particularly to two recent studies, those of Bright and Weinfeld.[66] According to Bright's list of the fifty-six cliches which occur five times or more, three occur in our passage: No. 22 "(to/with) you/we/thy and you/our/their fathers" (vs. 39); No. 23 "the land (place, city, inheritance) which I gave to you (them, your, their fathers) to you and your fathers" (vs. 39); No. 45 "to visit upon, punish" (vs. 34).[67] As for Weinfeld's list of deuteronomistic phraseology, there are two possibilities. His only claim for our text is No. 11c, "to cast off from before the face of Yahweh" (Jer 23:39). It should be noted that Weinfeld offers no other instances in which this particular phrase is used in the deuteronomistic material. The only other possible idiom is No. 21, "to become a reproach . . ." which is similar to Jer. 23:39.[68]

Do these instances of similarity in idiom strongly suggest that Jer 23:33-40 is part of the deuteronomistic prose tradition? One must answer both yes and no. One verse, vs. 39, represents three of the four claimed examples of deuteronomistic phraseology in the pericope. And yet, vs. 39 does not in any way develop the interpretation of $maśśā^{\circ}$; rather it is a separate judgment. Hence it is highly questionable whether Jer 23:39 should be used to decide the general date of style of the composition.

Furthermore, certain phraseology which we might expect to appear in a deuteronomistic discussion of "false prophecy" is quite markedly missing. Using Bright's collection, we might have expected No. 15, "certain constructions with nby³ym," or No. 19, "šqr in various constructions,"[69] the more so since, as Overholt has pointed out, reflection on šeqer was a very common if not definitive way in which the deuteronomistic Jeremianic prose tradition addressed the issue of false prophecy.[70]

Therefore the evidence for accepting Jer 23:34-40 as part of the early deuteronomistic prose on the grounds of phraseology is not overwhelming. Phrases we should expect do not appear and the phrases which do appear are found in one verse (vs. 39), thematically unrelated to the later exposition.

The second contention is also negative—Jer 23:34-40 does not share the form-critical characteristics which have been asserted for the C material by Nicholson and Thiel. Nicholson has suggested the literary structure of the prose in Jeremiah shares significant features with the covenant form as we find it in the deuteronomistic history.[71] Granting Nicholson's thesis for the sake of argument, Jer 23:34-40 does not appear to derive from or be influenced by ancient Near Eastern or Israelite contractual agreements. So too, the two basic deuteronomistic parenetic forms which Thiel has identified in the deuteronomistic literature, the *"Alternative- Predigt,"* a homiletic form, and the *"Gerichtsbegründung im Frage-Antwort-Stil,"* a catechetic form, are not present in this text.[72]

A third reason for suggesting that Jer 23:34-40 does not seem to be part of the early deuteronomistic prose centers on the way in which the problem of improper prophecy is treated. Much of the Jeremianic prose does treat of or concern the problem of false prophecy, but the narratives do more than just "concern" the problem, they attempt to resolve it. Hence we must be precise about how a given text deals with false prophecy.

Within the book of Jeremiah, we should first note the contrast between prose and poetic statements about the problem of prophecy. In the poetic oracles, prophets are indicted in rather vague terms; they prophesy falsely (Jer 5:31), act falsely (8:10; 6:13), or they do not have the word or knowledge of Yahweh (6:13; 23:14ff.). All this is in the form of summary condemnation leading up to predictions of judgment; the false prophets will be shamed. Those prophets who are guilty as charged will be punished.

Some of the Jeremianic prose carries on the same general condemnation which we found in the poetic material, i.e. "they speak lies" (Jer 29:8-9).[73] Texts admonish listeners not to listen or pay attention to those who prophesy falsely (Jer 23:16-17, 23-32). But the crucial issue in the prose material appears to be the method by which one may designate a prophet as false. The issue is not so much of condemnation as it is of resolving conflict or confrontation. Surely this interest represents a different approach to the problem of prophecy from that of summary condemnation which we observed in the poetic material.

Jeremiah 27-28 provide the best examples of how the prose traditionists thought one should cope with a confrontation between two prophets. In Jeremiah 27, the writer depicts a general opposition between those prophets, both Israelite and foreign, who predict that Nebuchadnezzar will not conquer the Syria-Palestinian states and who contradict Jeremiah, a prophet predicting the coming Babylonian victory. For the writer, the resolution of the conflict is simple, "Do not listen to the prophets who say . . ." (Jer 27:9, 14). False prophets may be immediately discerned and avoided on the basis of the content of their message.

This simplicity of approach is absent from the ensuing chapter, Jeremiah 28, which depicts a similiar confrontation as a virtually unresolvable problem. When Hananiah confronts Jeremiah with an oracle, Jeremiah's single option is to appeal to past prophetic performance in suggesting that Hananiah's words are untrue.[74] After this protest, Jeremiah is only able "to go his way" (Jer 28:11). When Jeremiah does receive a word directed to this specific situation, he goes and confronts Hananiah with the new oracle. For Jeremiah the problem was solved, but for the populace there would have been no way to adjudicate the validity or truth of the conflicting oracles. The prophetic performance of both Hananiah and Jeremiah was replete with classical Israelite prophetic trappings. Only with the death of Hananiah was the issue resolved—the true prophetic word had to be verified by later history.

Even in conflicts during which potentially confirmable words were spoken, the decision faced by the listener was difficult—he had to wait for confirmation. This method of verification was clearly valuable for the retrospective judgment of the Deuteronomist, e.g. Jer 37:19, "Where are your prophets who prophesied to you saying. . . ?"; but for those faced with a conflict which needed immediate resolution, there was no easy solution.

The book of Deuteronomy reflects much the same problem with prophecy as does Jeremiah, though Deuteronomy reflects a more systematic approach. In two places, the writer legislates the workings of Israelite prophecy. Deuteronomy 13 allows for easy solution of a simple case: if a prophet who predicts a sign which comes true says follow after other gods, then the listener shall know he is false. The evil prophet is to be put to death. The solution depends upon historical verification as well as upon knowing that the prophet in question has spoken on behalf of non-Israelite deities. Deuteronomy 13, however, ignores the more pointed problem of the case of false prophets who claim Yahweh as their god. Deuteronomy 18 proceeds to this case of a Yahweh prophet who does not speak Yahweh's words. Such a prophet is to die, though by whose hand is not specified.[75] The people will know if a prophet is false when his words do not come true. And once they know, the people may simply ignore him since "that prophet will die." This is the same problem and solution presented to us in Jeremiah 27—29. Yahweh will requite the false Yahwistic prophet; the people should just ignore him.[76]

In sum, Jer 23:34-40 treats false prophecy differently than does Deuteronomy and the Jeremianic prose narratives which reflect a unitary approach. Rather than adjudicate whether or not an oracle is valid, Jeremiah 23 argues for the elimination of new prophetic performance. As we shall see later, this different perspective reflects a new type of "false prophecy" which the post-exilic prophetic traditionists had encountered.

A fourth and final reason for thinking the wordplay using *maśśā°* to mean oracle is not from deuteronomistic hands rests precisely on the use of this word with identical meaning in the deutero-prophetic literature.[77] Since Zech 9:1; 12:1 and Mal 1:1 are collections headed by the label *maśśā°* meaning "oracle," it seems legitimate to infer that the similar use in Jer 23:34-40 reflects the same stylistic predilection, that of the prophetic traditionists.[78]

Having suggested that Jer 23:34-40 does not belong to the early deuteronomistic prose material, we raise an important question: to whom may we attribute this material? Some scholars have long recognized that certain portions of Jeremiah postdate the work of the deuteronomistic redactor of Jeremiah. For example, J. Hyatt suggested that a significant block of material, including Jer 23:34-40, may derive from a Persian-age (or later) redactor. [79] Nor is Jer 23:34-40 the only text which is post-Deuteronomy I and pre-Deuteronomy II, using the labels of E. Tov.[80] On the basis of idiom and theme, I would also assign Jer 3:15-18 to this same redactional period.[81] *lo° tizkerû ᶜôd* (Jer 23:36) and *lo° yō°merû ᶜôd* (Jer 3:16) are strikingly similar. Furthermore in Jer 3:15-18, the concern for the restoration of Israel and Judah, with Jerusalem as the focal point of the nations, is typical of early apocalyptic literature (cf. Zechariah, chapters 11 and 14).[82] Jer 23:34-40 is not the only example of late deutero-prophetic literature to be found in Jeremiah.

Perhaps no other book in the Hebrew Bible offers greater evidence of continuing redactional activity, activity of a rather consistent sort. The text-critical problems endemic to the study of Jeremiah are inexorably bound up with the redaction history of the book. As is well known, LXX has preserved a shorter version of the text of Jeremiah, particularly in the prose material often designated as deuteronomistic. Some of the deuteronomistic prose is shared by MT and LXX, i.e. the inclusion of some deuteronomistic material predates the characteristically prolix MT text type.[83] Much deuteronomistic prose material in MT is, however, missing in LXX, a fact which suggests that the redactional activity continued to take place after the LXX textual type achieved its form, i.e. probably late in the Persian period. Such evidence of late revision forces one to conclude that the book of Jeremiah underwent significant redaction over a period of several centuries.

E. Tov's work on the text and redaction-critical problems of Jeremiah buttresses this contention about the long period over which the Jeremianic prose was composed. He convincingly argues that the major redactional stages were spread over a lengthy period: I—the compiler of the LXX-length text, and II—the compiler-editor of the MT-length text.[84]

For our purposes, it is sufficient to note the long development in the Jeremianic redaction. The circles which produced this prose material were active over a broad span of time; especially if with Bright we are to identify them as responsible for the so-called biographical material, texts which give evidence of having been composed very near the time of Jeremiah himself.[85] Prose texts which deviate from the early and coherent deuteronomistic style are likely candidates for classification as a later part of the continuing redactional activity. Such is the case with Jer. 23:34-40.

In summary, we have discovered a deutero-prophetic text in the book of Jeremiah, a text which is an exegesis of a wordplay most probably going back to Jeremiah. The text was written later than the early deuteronomistic prose additions to the Jeremianic oracle collection. The purpose of this exegetical piece was to prohibit new oracles in the classical prophetic style; apparently people were improperly claiming to have words from Yahweh.

ii

A second deutero-prophetic text intensifies the negative assessment of prophecy we discovered in Jeremiah 23. To discern the nature of this anti-prophetic tradition, we now turn to an extremely difficult passage, Zech 13:2-6, a text which nonetheless has yielded significant results for this study.

Zechariah 13: 2-6

2 And it shall happen on that day, says the Lord of Hosts
    I will cut off the names of the idols from the land,
        and they shall no more be remembered, and
    I will purge[86] the prophets and the unclean spirit
        from the land.
3 And it shall happen, that if anyone should still prophesy,
        his father and his mother shall say to him;
        "You shall not live
        for you speak lies in the name of the Lord."
    And his father and mother shall kill[87] him when he prophesies.
4 And it shall happen on that day,
        every prophet shall be ashamed of his vision when he
            prophesies,[88]
    and they shall not put on a hairy mantle[89] in order to deceive,
5 but he shall say "I am no prophet
            I am a worker of the land;
            the land is my possession[90]
                from my youth."
6 And when one says to him,
        "What are these wounds on your back?"[91]
    He will answer,
        "That was when I was wounded in the house of my
            friends."[92]

My delimitation of these verses is based on the stylistic leitmotif in Zech 12-14, namely the formula "on that day," which holds together disparate material—descriptions of the traditionists' present concerns (as in Zech 13:2-6) and descriptions of the coming victory of Yahweh (as in Zech 14:1-4). The expression *bayyôm hahûʾ* occurs at the beginning of Zech 13:1, 2, and 4.

Although Zech 13:7 does not begin with this phrase, the developed shepherd imagery in vss. 7-9 denotes, as such imagery indicates in Zechariah 10 and 11, a different issue and strongly suggests that these verses were originally unrelated to Zech 13:2-6. Admittedly, the shepherd figure may be interpreted as prophetic or royal, although the latter is surely preferable. In either case, the concern for a restored remnant in Zech 13:7-9 points to a different interest than the more negative pronouncement in vss. 2-6.

To delimit this Yahweh speech should not blind us to the fact that this pericope about prophecy is a part of a larger and redactionally unified whole. Saebo has also pointed to the almost monotonous repetition of similar introductory formulae in Zech 12:2-13:6, the phrase *bayyôm hahûʾ*.[93] Also important in Zech 12:2-13:6 is the variation between Yahweh speech and prophetic speech, a technique which serves to emphasize the key sections of the composition: Zech 12:3; 12:9; and 13:2.[94] The various themes included in Zech 12:2-13:6 are varied, as is the whole of Deutero-Zechariah.[95]

Form-critical observations also provide valuable evidence. Zech 13:2 is a first-person legal sentence which usually occurs only at the conclusion of a judgment oracle.[96] In Zech 13:2, the sentence initiates the unit. Likewise unusual, there is no mention of the prophet as messenger. Yahweh himself is making the judgment; there is no intermediary. In vs. 3, we find what appears to be casuistic legal language, the "if . . . then" so common to ancient Near Eastern legal formulations. Zech 13:4-6 provides something akin to what Wildberger and Westermann have called prophetic accounts or reports.[97] Typically in these accounts, the prophet has the last word (cf. Amos 7:10ff.). However, here the account, instead of providing a prophetic word of judgment, depicts the past of the prophet as one of questionable motive and physical mutilation. The account is a word of self-judgment.

Having described these formal characteristics, we render our use of form-criticism counterproductive if we insist on an earlier oral configuration of these verses. There is no indication that such a tradition-complex existed. Instead classical categories appear to have been appropriated into a literary admixture for the purpose of denigrating the prophetic enterprise.

The allusions in Zech 13:2-6 run the gamut of Israel's prophetic experience: the ecstatic, the bemantled Elijah, the iconoclastic Amos. Zech 13:2 begins with the oft-stated prohibition against idols; interestingly the stricture is directed against the names and memory of idols. Such a law is hardly unique or surprising, especially when the prohibition against images and likenesses had been such an important part of Israel's heritage. But the addendum, that Yahweh hates the prophets as well as the unclean spirit *(hapax)*, creates the new polemic. To discover that this combined polemic against prophet and spirit was not a universal view in post-exilic times, we need only refer to the Chronicler's description of Joash's reign in 2 Chron 24:18ff. The people served Asherim and ʿaṣabbîm whereupon prophets were sent to save the people.

Zechariah 13:2-3 appears to draw directly upon Deuteronomic concerns. The threat in Zech 13:2 echoes the repeated use of a formula to be found in Deuteronomy, *ûbîᶜartā hārāᶜ miqqirbekā* (Deut 17:7; 19:9; 21:21; 22:21, 24; 24:7, and especially Deut 13:6 where it refers specifically to the apostate prophet).[98] Zech 13:2 also seems to reflect the violent expunging of improper religious practice as that is presented in Deut 12:3. Zech 13:3 also shares Deuteronomic concerns, specifically as those are found in Deut 13:1-11 and 21:18-21. The warrant whereby parents receive authority derives, of course, from one of the basic commandments. However, this parental authority and its extent were more fully spelled out in Deut 21:18-21. The nature of the recalcitrant offspring is specified: disobedient, stubborn, rebellious, gluttonous, drunken. In the Deuteronomic case, the parents were to turn over the son for prosecution and punishment. In Zechariah, the parents act as prosecutor, judge, and executioner. The obvious implication is that the nature of this transgression—prophesying—is much more serious than the disobedient son and requires immediate extermination. The further implication that anyone who prophesies is immature, subject to one's elders, and not protected by normal judicial procedures, can hardly be interpreted as a favorable overview of prophetic activity. Furthermore, the Zechariah polemic appears to be based exegetically upon Deut 13:1-11. The general indictment of prophecy in Zechariah takes its cue from the Deuteronomic prohibition of paganizing mantic activity and apostasy in general; so especially Deut 13:7-9 as these verses constitute a similar method of punishment to that prescribed in Zechariah 13. Zech 13:6 "What are these wounds on your back?" also seems to reflect a deuteronomic prohibition, 14:1 "You shall not cut yourselves."

Within the "bad son" legal framework, we might expect to find the formal Deuteronomic charge against bad prophets: if what he says does not come true, he shall die (Deut 18:15ff.); or the further refinement in Deut 13:2ff., that if the prophecy does come true, but the prophet is speaking on behalf of another god, he shall die. Instead, the writer appeals to the *šeqer* language, derivative of the prophetic conflicts in Jeremiah (Jer 14:14; 23:25; 29:21). A striking example is the accusation made by Jeremiah against prophets and other diviners of weal in Jeremiah 27:8-11. Here the prophets have recommended resistance against Babylon. Jeremiah argues that these words are lies "with the result that you will be removed from the land, and I will drive you out and you will perish"—very nearly the same argument employed here in Zechariah (if one reads ᵓᶜbyr in vs. 2). However, in Zechariah, the sentence will fall not on the people but on those prophets who spoke falsely in Yahweh's name. The sentence has been switched from the people to the prophets.

šqr language is used in a special nexus. Speaking *šqr* is to break the covenant which governs human action (Exod 20:16; Deut 19:8). Those who swear falsely incur the curses enjoined for breach of covenant. In the Sefire treaty, if either party should *yšqr,* the curses would be activated.[99] Men may break the covenant, but the treaty has divine authorization and therein lies the source and force of the curses.[100]

As we move to Zech 13:4, the allusions to Israel's traditions continue. Immediately, the prophetic enterprise is thrown into question when the mode of prophecy is limited to visions. In the Jeremianic critique (Jer 23:16) the false prophets are speaking "visions of their own minds, not from the mouth of the Lord." These are prophecies of a second-rate genre. Further, the theme of shame, *yēbōšû*, harks back to the threat against earlier purveyors of welfare. Micah 3:5-8 gives an oracle against such *šālôm* prophets. One of the threats is that they will be ashamed of their visions. The corollary threat is that the prophets will have nothing to say; Yahweh will give them no answer; they will not be prophets.

The *'adderet śē'ār* complicates matters because we think immediately of the prophetic mantle of Elijah and Elisha (I Kgs 19:19; 2 Kgs 2:13). The Elisha and Elijah cycles would have called to mind legitimate prophetic activity (2 Kgs 2:8, 14). How then might this mantle constitute an anti-prophetic polemic? One may, I think, point to the use of the term to describe Esau in Gen 25:25. By using such a hairy mantle Jacob was able to deceive Isaac and gain Esau's birthright. Such an allusion to Israel's early epic heritage would have been a distinct option to post-exilic traditionists and thus could have provided a tie between prophecy and deceptive technique.

The famous disclaimer of Amos 7:14 is surely the source of vs. 5. Nevertheless the use of this same phrase, *lô' nābî' 'ānōkî*, is unclear in our passage, as is the nature of the final claim, *'ādām hiqnani*. As indicated above, Otzen's attempt to link the MT with the Targum and Peshitta root *qn'* seems unsatisfactory, though it would offer a valuable parallel for interpreting vs. 6.

A presupposition in the analysis thus far has been that vss. 2-6 are a basic unit. This view is not universally accepted. "And on that day," the stylistic *leitmotif* of Zech 12:2—13:6 recurs in vss. 2 and 4 giving at least some reason to think that more than one element is involved. One might argue that there is a difference in content between the two sections; vss. 2-3 have to do with removal and punishment of prophets, while vss. 4-6 are more concerned with self-ostracism. These differences are slight though; and the theme of prophecy carries through consistently, as the presence of *hann⁰bî'îm*, perhaps as catch-words, in both vss. 2 and 4 shows.

Elliger suggests that vss. 2-3 comprise an original oracle about the death of certain prophets while vss. 4-6 are a later addition.[101] Saebo is more inclined to think that the unit, vss. 2-6, is the result of a "successive growth process," which is based upon an earlier saying (vs. 2).[102] Saebo's view is reasonable except that we have no internal evidence to demonstrate the successive character of this growth. Rather, because of the richness of the allusion to prior traditions about prophecy, I argue that Zech 13:2-6 is a conscious exegetical use of statements about and allusions to prophecy. The unit is a devastating polemic against everything prophetic.[103]

There have been many suggestions about the addressee of this piece.[104] Early on, many felt that the pre-exilic false prophets were indicated and consequently that the composition was pre-exilic (e.g. König, 1893). More recently, some have argued that not false prophets, but prophets in general are under attack (Sellin, 1929; Horst, 1954). Otzen thinks that exegetes like Mitchell (ICC) walk a middle road when they say "the word prophet was (in post-exilic times) almost synonymous with false prophet."[105] Otzen himself concludes that the author is attacking syncretistic prophets.[106] He thinks that this problem was paramount in pre-exilic times, but that passages like Neh 6:10-14 point out that similar problems occurred in the post-exilic community (though this text hardly proved his point). Basing his analysis on Janssen's reconstruction of exilic Israel, Otzen contends that the polemic derives from a religious degeneration when "heathen mantics flared up in Judah," most probably as a result of traffic with the Northern population.[107]

Otzen's solution seems attractive because the supposed syncretistic prophecy fits the composite nature of the passage. But this is also his crucial error. Just because the pericope is comprised of and refers to disparate elements does not mean that the attack is directed against a group that is doing all those things. On the basis of the above analysis, I would suggest that instead of reflecting syncretistic prophets, the author is attacking some form of post-exilic prophecy by culling the literary sources for ammunition. Otzen's impression of syncretistic, heathen mantics is really a tribute to the invective launched by the prophetic traditionist.

It is possible to theorize the object of this polemic. Paul Hanson has suggested:

> The passage is intriguing as evidence that the age of prophecy had passed and that those who claimed to be prophets were in fact false prophets. This explains why the visionary group, though the true successors of the prophets, refused to designate themselves as $n^e b\hat{i}^{\circ}\hat{i}m$.[108]

We have seen here how the "intriguing" quality of the passage was achieved by the exegetical-allusive work on earlier Israelite traditions. And we will discover in our investigation of Chronicles the identity of the group who claimed to be prophets in this period, the Levitical singers. A claim of this sort would have been repugnant to traditionists who preserved the words of earlier prophets. And if the traditionists represented different cultic tradi-tions—non-Jerusalemite—such friction would have added even more heat to the strife.

In summary, Jeremiah 23:33-40 and Zech 13:2-6 are deutero-prophetic texts denigrating prophetic activity. Jeremiah 23 represents a move beyond the conflict with false prophets as described in Deuteronomy and in Jeremianic prose and constitutes a late interpretation of a Jeremianic word-play about the people as $ma\acute{s}\acute{s}\bar{a}^{\circ}$. Zech 13:2-6, a pericope which has been incorporated into the booklet Zechariah 12—14, attempts to expunge all prophets as unclean. Both texts probably derive from a period, the late sixth or early fifth century, in which prophetic traditionists were confronted with some other group who claimed to be prophets. Their response was to argue that prophetic performance in the classical mold was a thing of the past, and any attempts at prophetic performance were to be rejected.

D. Prophecy in the Future

On the basis of the harsh words directed at prophecy in Jer 23:34-40 and Zech 13:2-6, we might expect a consistently negative attitude toward prophetic performance within the entire deutero-prophetic corpus. Not so. Consistent with, and perhaps depending upon, the furturity of the prophet-servant in Deutero-Isaiah, in both the books of Joel and Malachi we find an expectation for prophecy to return in the future. Conjecture about a precise date for this material yields no firm results. I suggest a date no later than the beginning of the Hellenistic period.[109]

i

The first text to be examined is Joel 3:1-5.

1 And then it shall happen, [110]
    I will pour out my spirit[111] upon all flesh;
    Your sons and your daughters shall be prophets,[112]
    Your old men shall dream dreams,
    Your young men shall see visions.
2 Even upon[113] the menservants and maidservants
    I will in those days pour out my spirit.
3 I will set signs in the heavens and on the earth
    blood and fire; and columns of smoke.[114]
4 The sun will be turned to darkness
      and the moon to blood,
    before the day of the Lord comes
      which is a terrible and great thing.
5 And all who call upon the name of the Lord[115]
        will be saved;
      because there will be salvation on Mount Zion
        as the Lord said
      and survivors whom Yahweh will summon.[116]

Before examining the place of this pericope in the development of a theory about prophecy, we must take note of its place in the book of Joel. There is a good bit of controversy on this latter point. Plöger has argued that chapter 3, along with chapter 4, is part of an eschatological section, but that Joel 3 is later than chapter 4.[117] Rudolph, who thinks Joel to be a unified product, suggests that chapters 3 and 4 comprise an integrated subsection.[118] Wolff gives the most detailed analysis, and asserts that Joel 2:18—3:5 comprises a large assurance oracle *(Erhörungszuspruch)* of which Joel 3:1-5 makes up three smaller sections: vss. 1-2 oracle of salvation *(Heilszuspruch)*, vss. 3-4 announcement of a sign *(Zeichenansage)*, vs. 5 announcement of salvation

(Heilsansage).[119] Wolff's proposals seem to be the most adequate way to classify 3:1-5; but his arguments for a structural connection between chapters 2 and 3 seem weak. That much of the book is a highly exegetical literary product, making eclectic use of older prophetic literature, is now certain.[120] But that the entire book is a literary unit is dubious, especially because of its exegetical and eclectic character.

A more tangled problem is the inner coherence of Joel 3:1-5. That vss. 1-2 belong together is suggested by the similarity in theme as well as the root *špk* which opens and closes the verses. Likewise, vss 3-4 evince a homogeneity of symbolism in chiastic order. Vs. 5 acts, so Wolff has noted, as an announcement of salvation for those called and for Zion. Rather than argue for a unity of text on form-critical grounds, as Wolff has done, I suggest that what we have here is a description of the preliminaries to the eschatological age, a part of the eschatological scenario, or as Rudolph puts it, preliminary signs of the final age.[121]

One of the pressing questions posed by this text is that of its futuristic connotation. When are these signs to be manifest? We have three phrases which are susceptible to a temporal interpretation. The first, *wᵉhāyāh ʾaḥᵃrê-kēn* is surely to be read as an editorial connecting piece, a "connecting formula."[122] The *bayyāmîm hāhēmmāh* of vs. 2 is commonly used in Jeremiah, in both oracles of weal and woe, to point to the future: Jer 3:16, 18; 5:18; 31:29; 33:15, 16; 50:4, 20; and also Zech 8:23. One might want to argue that the phrase denotes the eschatological age, as in Jer 31:15ff.; but to contend that the phrase is an eschatological *terminus technicus* is probably to overstate the case. In vs. 4 we meet the much discussed *yôm yhwh,*[123] a phrase which probably derives from holy war formulations.[124]

To launch immediately into a discussion of what constitutes the Day of Yahweh would ignore the particularity of the Joel text. The extraordinary signs are to occur *lipnê,* before the day of Yahweh comes. Once we recognize the "pre"-quality of vs. 4, vs. 5 makes more sense; for we are talking about the conditions for a successful existence through the fateful day of Yahweh. We have to do with part of the eschatological scenario: *praeparatio.* This is part of what is to happen before Yahweh works his victory and reestablishes a visible kingship on Zion. These five verses contain themes and motifs gathered from earlier Israelite literature and traditions which are now used to describe the coming days.

Three individual elements are of paramount importance: the pouring out of the spirit, the cosmic signs, and salvation on Zion. In vss. 1-2, the writer has synthesized thoughts about a pouring out of the spirit with the return of prophecy for the whole people. Because of the divine *rûaḥ,* all Israel will become prophets. Aside from the uses of *špk* for pouring out of the spirit in Joel, we find the phrase used in Ezek 39:29 and Zech 12:10, two other deutero-prophetic texts.[125] In both places, this pouring is used to describe the coming day of Yahweh.[126] In Zechariah 12, a spirit of grace and supplication will be poured out upon the house of David. In Ezekiel 39, Yahweh will pour out his spirit to demonstrate his presence with Israel.[127] At these places in the description of the coming age, the pouring out of the spirit was not explicitly tied to the return of prophecy; in Joel the pouring out of the spirit is, however, linked to the return of prophecy as a sign of Yahweh's coming beneficence.

That the return of prophecy was seen as a good sign and not a curse, we may infer from the implied reference to Num 11:29.[128] Moses, when confronted with the activity of Eldad and Medad, is reported to have said, "Would that all the people were prophets, that the Lord would put his spirit upon them." Even at this stage there was a conjunction between Yahweh's bestowal of spirit and consequent prophecy. The Numbers text provides the conceptual raw material for the contention that a pouring out of the spirit will result in prophetic gifts for all Israel. The Joel text functions as an answer to the rhetorical question of Moses. The unclean spirit generating evil prophets (Zech 13:2-6) is an obvious contrast to the prophetic spirit of Yahweh which will be poured out upon Israel in the future. Joel 3:1 also provides a contrast with certain texts in Chronicles (2 Chr 15:1; 20:14; 24:20) which describe the bestowal of the spirit as the gift of prophetic certainty, a gift which the Chronicler contends has been given to the Levitical prophets and a gift which the Deutero-Joel author argues is only to be manifest in the future.[129]

Vss. 3-4 give another way of describing what will happen in the coming days: cosmic signs will be placed in the heavens. Joel 2:10 records a similar darkening of the sun and moon, as does Isa 13:10 where the darkness is part of the description of the day of Yahweh (see also Amos 5:18, 20; Joel 2:2; 4:15). But fire, columns of smoke and a blood-colored moon have been added to the scene in Joel 3:3-4.

One way to attempt to understand these signs is to search for origins. Are the fire and smoke taken from the theophanic description (Exod 19:18)? Are the signs an indication of Yahweh's presence in Zion (Isa 4:5)? Do they represent sacrifices on behalf of Yahweh?[130] Jeremias argues that the darkness imagery belonged originally to the day of Yahweh traditions.[131] The turning of the moon to blood, representing massive carnage, could be a logical inference from another component of the day of Yahweh tradition, the destruction of mankind.[132] I am more inclined to see the reddening of the moon as an expression of a more universal mythic motif, that of the relationship of the moon and blood. For example, Heiler says, "The moon directly affects human life, it is considered as the cause of menstruation and sickness."[133] Whatever the mythological or traditio-historical background of the moon changing to blood, the appearance of blood was to become a stock item in later apocalyptic visions (Rev 6:13; Mark 13:24; Matt 24:29). Joel was the first to combine the blood imagery with the darkening traditions of the day of Yahweh.

The final clause of Joel 3:4, "before the day of the Lord comes which is a terrible and great thing," demonstrates yet another definitive characteristic of the book's scenario *praeparatio*. The adjectives "great and very terrible" are also used in Joel 2:11 to describe the day of Yahweh. Joel 3:4, however, provides a striking innovation; it introduces *lipnê*. The signs are preparatory to the coming of the day of Yahweh. This is no isolated conception, since the same clause appears in Mal 3:23, a text which describes Elijah's arrival occurring before Yahweh's theophany.

The final piece of this collection, vs. 5, in the form of a prophetic speech, is united by the roots for speaking, *qr²* and *²mr*. This promise of salvation includes another traditional element of the eschatological scenario—the partial salvation in Zion after an attack by the nations.[134] That we are here dealing with a mixture of Zion traditions as well as the day of Yahweh material, exemplified particularly in Obad:15a, 16-18, is clear. The Obadiah text is relevant: vs. 17, "but in Mount Zion there shall be those that escape. . . ."[135] Recognizing this background, we discover that vs. 5 functions as a contrast to the picture of universal benefit depicted in the earlier part of the oracle. Joel 3:1-2 gives a picture of all Israel receiving the gift of prophecy, whereas Joel 3:5a suggests that only those who call on the name of Yahweh will be saved. Vs. 5b goes even further in stating that only those in Zion will escape, and culminates with vs. 5c in which only those who are called by Yahweh will survive.

One is tempted to suggest that the lack of universality of the salvation is integrally connected to the dialectical nature of the day of Yahweh tradition in the later period. It was an event that threatened both the foreign nations and Israel herself: Zechariah 14 and Joel 1:15; 2:1, 11 depict the day of Yahweh against Israel whereas in Joel 3:4; 4:14 it is directed primarily against the nations. This represents a melding of earlier holy war (against the nations, Isa 13:6ff.) and prophetic traditions (against Israel, Amos 5:18a).[136]

The key to understanding the partiality of the salvation on Zion is the "calling" theme. But how are we to understand this dual calling—man on Yahweh and Yahweh on man? To call upon Yahweh's name is a fairly common idiom in the Old Testament. Texts like I Kgs 18:24 show there is a direct connection between calling on the name of Yahweh and allegiance to Jerusalem and Zion (cf. also Isa 12:4; Ps 105:1 in the cultic sphere). But even more, it appears that this calling on the name of the Lord is a part of the eschatological scenario (Zech 13:9; Isa 41:25). The Zechariah text is very important since we find there a chiastic presentation of the double calling which we found in Joel 3:5: "They will call on my name and I will answer them; I will say they are my people; and they will say, the Lord is my God" (Zech 13:9).[137] This text is particularly relevant in explaining the Joel passage since the context of Zech 13:7-9 is also that of a remnant being saved, this time from a refining fire. The argument in both the Joel and Zechariah texts is the same—that in the coming day of Yahweh, only some will be chosen. They must call on Yahweh, and they will be called by Yahweh.

These five verses are a part of the eschatological scenario, and as such, they have striking parallels to similar traditions in other deutero-prophetic texts. Secondly, consistent with an essential characteristic of deutero-prophetic literature, the Joel text is built upon earlier traditions whose stages we can identify in Ezek 39:29 and Obad vs. 17. There are three stock items: the pouring out of the spirit, the cosmic signs, and salvation on Zion. Each has been revised or presented in a new way, e.g. the moon-to-blood revision. Further, these traditions have been presented in such a way as to constitute a preparation for the coming day of Yahweh. Prophecy and cosmic signs will precede this event. And most important for the purposes of this study, the text allows an interpretation consistent with what we discovered in Zech 13:2-6. The present age is to be without prophecy. Prophecy is something to be polemicised. Only in the days to come may we speak of prophecy as legitimate, and then only in the context of the eschatological scenario depicting the prerequisites for the appearance of Yahweh.

ii

Perhaps the best rationale for ending this chapter with a brief look at Malachi is that it presents us with "the missing link."[138] Up to this point in our examination of various traditions and prophetic collections, we have discovered an expectation for the return of prophecy for an elect portion of Israel. But this expectation of prophecy returning in corporate fashion is a step away from the traditions of Qumran, the New Testament, and the Rabbinic literature. The collection of Malachi provides evidence for the focus of this expectation on an individual.[139]

The reasons for treating this prophetic collection in conjunction with the Joel text are as follows: both describe the coming day of Yahweh; both have a pointed concern for the preliminaries: what is to precede the appearance of Yahweh; both use similar phraseology: "the great and terrible day of Yahweh;" and both refer to the return of prophecy in the future. Hence, the book of Malachi gives every indication of belonging to the same theological stream as does Joel 3-4.

To turn to Malachi is to move from the expectation of the return of prophecy to the expectation of a coming figure. There are two classical texts: Mal 3:1 and vss. 23-24, the expectation of *malʾākî* and Elijah. To be dogmatic about Mal 3:1 would be unwise. In this Yahweh speech, we are told that a messenger, the prophetic "author" of the book, is to be sent before Yahweh arrives. Vss. 1-5, with the exception of "and the Lord whom you seek will come suddenly into his temple," apparently all refer to the action of this *malʾākî*. He is a judging figure whose work of purification will allow the requisite purity of cult for Yahweh to appear. The action of this messenger is defined by his cleansing of the Levites.[140] Only when the Levites have been cleansed, and the offerings of Israel are thus acceptable, will Yahweh himself draw near in judgment.

From a form-critical perspective, the messenger appears in one of the disputation-words of the book.[141] The argument of the people is disbelief in divine justice. The writer refutes this argument by predicting the coming of the messenger of the covenant.

The most serious argument that could be raised against our analysis is this: how does one justify describing the *maPākÎ* as a prophet? There is an alternative. The writer could be referring to the theophanic angel of the Elohistic accounts (Genesis 16; Numbers 22; Judges 6; 13). Actually, this possible objection provides the starting point for understanding the significance of this passage. In the Book of the Covenant (Exod 23:20-21) too, the messenger of Yahweh appears. The relationship between Mal 3:1 and Exod 23:20 is too striking to be accidental:

Mal 3:1   Behold I send my messenger
             he will prepare the way before me . . .
Exod 23:20 Behold I send my messenger   (reading with SP, LXX, V, and vs. 23)
             before you
             to guard your way . . .

This latter messenger is:

. . . to bring you to the place which I have prepared. Give heed to him and hearken to his voice, do not rebel against him, for he will not pardon your transgression for my name is in him. But if you hearken attentively to his voice and do all that I say, then I will be an enemy to your enemies and an adversary to your adversaries. (Exod 23:20-22)

The coming help of Yahweh by means of the messenger thus depends upon Israel's obedience to the laws of the Book of the Covenant. In Malachi, the coming of Yahweh depends upon the arrival of the messenger who will function as a covenant enforcer.[142] The passage in Malachi appears to be a reworking of the *mal°āk* text in the Book of the Covenant.

This exegetical or allusive enterprise also incorporates a theme common to other post-exilic prophetic traditionists in which messenger language is used to denote a type of prophetic activity. Deutero-Isaiah defines the servant activity with the appellation "messenger":

Isa 42:19   Who is blind but my servant
            or deaf as my messenger whom I send?
Isa 44:26   Who confirms the word of his servant,
            and performs the counsel of his messengers?

The book of Haggai evinces this same proclivity: "Haggai the messenger of the Lord" (Hag 1:13) in place of the more typical phrase in the book, "Haggai the prophet."

This prophetic connotation of "messenger" in post-exilic writings is not limited to the eschatological stream, for we find it in the Chronicler's history as well:

The Lord, the God of their fathers, sent persistently to them by his messengers, because he had compassion on his people and on his dwelling place; but they kept mocking the messengers of God, despising his words and scoffing at his prophets, till the wrath of the Lord rose against his people, till there was no remedy. (2 Chron 36:15-16)

The *mal³āk* of Exodus has been inserted into a conceptual environment in which such a figure was understood to be prophetic.

There are probably several reasons why a prophet was deemed necessary to appear before Yahweh came to stand in judgment. It was part of a more general expectation for the return of prophecy, an expectation consistent with the Joel text. But more importantly, Israel had already seen the prophets appear prior to judgment by Yahweh, the threats before the defeat of 587. Such is the sum and substance of the Chronicler's observation on the place of Israel's earlier prophets. They had come to warn the nation. Yahweh then appeared in judgment; and since Israel had not repented, his judgment fell on them. The Chronicler observed that the prophets preceded Yahweh's coming, that they had attempted to prepare the people for it. Now this memory was turned into an expectation for prophecy to precede Yahweh's appearance on his day.

If the precursant messenger of Mal 3:1 is a prophetic figure, how are we to interpret the final two verses of the book? That they are, along with vs. 22, late addenda to the book is universally recognized. In all probability, vss. 23-24 are the third ending of the collection, "says the Lord of Hosts" comprising the first (3:21), and the appeal to Mosaic piety the second (3:22).

Since we have discovered the idea of a coming prophetic figure in Joel 2:17-3:5, we have *prima facie* reason to think that there is at least thematic similarity between vss. 23-24 and that earlier passage. Eissfeldt has, I think, caught part of the significance of this addition: "Mal 3:23-24, however, are intended to make precise the proclamation of 3:1, of a heavenly messenger who is to precede Yahweh when he appears for judgment, and to correct this by indicating that Elijah is this messenger."[143] According to this view, vss. 23-24 provide a specification of the earlier expectation. There was a prophet, who, because he did not die, was available for such a reappearance (e.g. 2 Kgs 2:11 and also Enoch 89:52).

The pericope, Mal 3:23-24, is however, more than just an identification of this coming prophet. It continues the theme of the eschatological scenario; the prophet will come as a part of the *praeparatio* for the day of Yahweh. Malachi uses the same phrase as Joel 3:4, "before the great and terrible day of the Lord comes." The coming of the prophet in Malachi occupies the same syntactic position as do the sun turning to darkness and the moon to blood in Joel. The theme of the sons and fathers is probably less a matter of appeal to texts like Mic 7:17 but more a typical manner of speaking in certain eschatological texts, the resolution of opposites. Both Joel 3:1, the sons, daughters, and fathers prophesy, and Mal 3:24, the mutuality of fathers and sons, demonstrate this theme. And this theme functions less as an ethical imperative than as a way of describing the period just prior to the arrival of Yahweh in the eschatological age (e.g. Isa 3:5; Mic 7:17; Jer 9:1-5 for the theme in earlier prophetic books and more importantly the development of this theme in Jub 23:16-21).[144] The curse, vs. 24b, recognizes the possibility that the prophet will be unable to create the requisite ritual and ethical cleanliness for Yahweh's coming to be safe for Israel.

To summarize what I have said about the texts in Jeremiah, Deutero-Zechariah, Joel, and Malachi is to observe what the writers of the deutero-prophetic collections after 520 B.C. thought about Israelite prophecy, its problems and its future. What they said may be put as follows: classical Israelite prophecy was a thing of the past and claims for contemporary manifestations of prophecy were to be denied. The appropriate task for prophetic traditionists was not to be prophets but was instead to reflect on the earlier prophetic words and to interpret them for their own age. Such work was performed by prophetic traditionists who placed their compositions, the deutero-prophetic literature, within the collections of the classical prophets. These writers expected prophecy to return as a necessary sign of the times just prior to Yahweh's theophany in the *yôm yhwh*. This return was conceived of as a return of prophecy for all the people and as the return of a single prophetic figure. Both expectations lived on as viable traditions, as Acts 2 and Matt 17:10 demonstrate.

[1] I. Willi-Plein, *Vorformen der Schriftexegese innerhalb des Alten Testaments. Untersuchungen zum literarischen Werden der auf Amos, Hosea, und Micha zurückgehenden Bücher im hebräischen Zwölfprophetenbuch* (BZAW 123; Berlin: W. de Gruyter, 1971) 36.

[2] *Ibid.* 244-247. See recently R. Clements, *Prophecy and Tradition* (Oxford: Blackwell, 1974) 41-57 who argues for an integral relationship between classical prophetic books and the deuteronomistic view of prophecy.

[3] The relation of expansionistic text types (e.g. MT of Jeremiah and MT, 1QIsa of Isaiah) to earlier strata of interpretation is complex and only now beginning to be studied. See for example, E. Tov, "L'incidence de la critique textuelle sur la critique littéraire dans le livre de Jérémie," *RB* 79 (1972) 189-199, and M. Goshen-Gottstein, "Hebrew Syntax and the History of the Biblical Text," *Textus* 8 (1973) 100-106.

[4] Apart from the two examples cited in the text, other examples would include S. Frost, *Old Testament Apocalyptic* (London: Epworth, 1952), 112ff.; D. Russell, *The Method and Message of Jewish Apocalyptic* (Philadelphia: Westminster, 1964) 184-187; M. Delcor, "Les Sources du Deutero-Zacharie et ses procédés d'emprunt," *RB* 59 (1952) 385-411; Plöger, *Theocracy and Eschatology,* 110; R. North, Prophecy to Apocalyptic via Zechariah, *VT Supp* 22, 54. F. Bruce, "The Earliest Old Testament Interpretation," *Oud St* 17 (1972) 38-40.

[5] P. Grech, "Interprophetic Re-Interpretation and Old Testament Eschatology," *Augustinianum* 9 (1969) 242-243.

[6] S. Paul, "Literary and Ideological Echoes of Jeremiah in Deutero-Isaiah," *Proceedings of the Fifth World Congress of Jewish Studies* (Jerusalem: World Union of Jewish Studies, 1972) 102-120.

[7] I am not the first to observe a pattern or schema in certain of these texts. Paul Hanson, building upon Cross's observations in "The Divine Warrior" (*CMHE,* 91-111, has argued for the

existence of a mythic pattern which, in the Israelite material, receives the label, Divine Warrior Hymn, cf. Hanson's "Zechariah 9 and the Recapitulation of an Ancient Ritual Pattern," *JBL* 92 (1973) 37-59.

[8]Cf. D. Hillers, *Treaty-Curses and the Old Testament Prophets* (Rome: Pontifical Biblical Institute, 1964) and D. McCarthy, *Treaty and Covenant, A Study in Form in the Ancient Oriental Documents and in the Old Testament* (Rome: Pontifical Biblical Institute, 1963).

[9]On the relation of Zechariah to apocalyptic, apart from the works of Hanson and North already cited, see most recently S. Amsler, "Zacharie et l'origine de l'apocalyptique" *VT Supp* 22, 226-231, and H. Gese, "Anfang und Ende der Apokalyptik, dargestellt am Sacharjabuch," *ZTK* 70 (1973) 20-49.

[10]J. Lindblom, *Die Jesaja-Apokalypse* (LUA 34.3; Lund: Gleerup, 1938) 67-69. Cf. also Willi-Plein who makes much the same argument on the basis of the doxologies in Amos, *Vorformen der Schriftexegese,* 66.

[11]That Isaiah 24—27 and 34—35 are part of the deutero-prophetic material, I do not deny. These chapters, however, provide little explicit evidence about the prophetic task.

[12]P. Volz contends that Deutero-Isaiah contains the substance of worship, *Jesaia II* (Leipzig: A. Deichertsche Buchhandlung, 1932).

[13]C. Westermann, *Isaiah 40-66* (Philadelphia: Westminster, 1969) 6.

[14]Isa 48:16d is probably secondary; Westermann, *Isaiah,* 203; J. Muilenburg, "The Book of Isaiah, Chapters 40-66," *IB,* Vol. 5 (New York: Abingdon, 1956) 429.

[15]Reading *w⁾wmrh* with IQIsa*ᵃ* instead of *w⁾mr* as in M, S, T Ps J. LXX and V are ambiguous. *W⁾wmr* is itself difficult. The proclivity to read *w⁾wmrh* as a first person form is puzzling. To defend this interpretation one would need to theorize a cohortative form, a suggestion which makes little sense in this context. *w⁾wmrh* is better understood to be a qal fem. sg. participle, an interpretation I owe to S. Dean McBride. Such an interpretation accords well with the context, which is an admonition to the prophetess in the divine council, "Speak tenderly to Jerusalem," (Isa 40:1) and the direct address to Zion, "Get you up to a high mountain, O Zion," (Isa 40:9). Cf. F. Cross *CMHE,* 188.

Prof. McBride has, in a recent, private communication, added greater detail to the argument that *w⁾wmrh* is a qal fem. sg. participle. (1) The qal act. fem. sg. participle appears once in the Massoretic text of Isaiah (47:8—with reference, interestingly, to personified Babylon) where it is written *h⁾mrh,* i.e. the usual defective orthography. In IQIsa*ᵃ*, this form occurs as *h⁾wmrh,* i.e. the plene orthography. (2) There are five occurrences of *w⁾mr* (*waw* consecutive plus first person sg. impf. qal) in M of Isaiah. In attesting these forms, IQIsa*ᵃ* twice exhibits *w⁾mr* (6:5; 24:16); the remaining three occurrences are rendered in IQIsa*ᵃ* as sg. cohortatives, written simply *w⁾mrh* in 6:8, 11, while in 41:9 a plene *waw* has been added (either by the original scribe or a later corrector) as a supralinear correction: *w⁾ʷmrh.* (3) There is an obvious problem in supposing that IQIsa*ᵃ* preserves a more original fem. sg. participle since the preceding imperative, apparently addressed to the figure who responds, would seem to be masc. sg. in IQIsa*ᵃ* as well as in M. This too is a complicated issue since the orthography and pronunciation of the fem. sg. impert. of *qr⁾* are uncertain. The standard paradigms suggest *qr⁾y* (*qir⁾î*), though the only supporting evidence appears to derive from roots which are "weak" in some other respect (in addition to final ⁾), e.g. *bō⁾î, ṣ⁾î, š⁾î.* Given the assimilation of final ⁾ verbs with final *w/y* roots in Semitic generally, one wonders if *q⁾rî⁾* is appropriate. According to Ziegler's LXX notes, there is an Aquila marginal gloss for *qr⁾* in Isa 40:6, giving the transliteration *kria[i],* a form which certainly looks more like a fem. imperative than a masc. one (M, *q⁾rā⁾*). (4) The original text of Isa 40:6a may have read: *qwl ⁾mr qr⁾y w⁾mrh mh ⁾qr⁾* (or *qwl ⁾mr qr⁾y ⁾mrh mh ⁾qr⁾*). The confusion attested in later texts and versions, and interpretations, could have resulted from haplography and/or misreading of consonants (*waw* and *yodh* were often confused in the paleo-Hebrew script). The obvious parallel in Isa 6:5, 8, 11, where the first person is clear, may well have been the primary factor informing the reading of V and LXX. (Note that neither LXX nor V distinguishes mas. and fem. sg. imperatives, offering no help on the original reading of "call/proclaim.") It is significant that M resisted the strong attraction of the Isa 6 parallel, apparently taking the subject of *w⁾mr* to be an angelic voice (so Ibn Ezra, and cf. Isa 6:3 and 1 Kgs 22:20). Then too the syntax of Isa 40:1ff. does not lead us to expect the sudden appearance of a *waw* consecutive form.

[16]N. Habel, "The Form and Significance of the Call Narrative," *ZAW* 77 (1965) 314ff.

[17]*Ibid.* 317. F. Cross' emphasis on the place of the divine council should also keep us from interpreting Isa 40:6 as biography, "The Council of Yahweh in Second Isaiah," *JNES* 12 (1953) 274-275.

[18]Muilenburg, "The Book of Isaiah," 429.

[19]Westermann, *Isaiah,* 7, 131ff.; Muilenburg, "The Book of Isaiah," 397.

[20]Westermann, *Isaiah,* 23.

[21]O. Eissfeldt, "The Promises of Grace to David in Isaiah 55:1-5," *Israel's Prophetic Heritage,* 203.

[22]*Ibid.* 204.

[23]Volz, *Jesaia II,* 140; Westermann, *Isaiah,* 283; Muilenburg, "The Book of Isaiah," 646; von Rad, *Old Testament Theology,* Vol. 2, 240; J. McKenzie, *Second Isaiah* (Garden City: Doubleday, 1968) 144.

[24]For a similar view on the decreasing importance of the Davidic tradition in Deutero-Isaiah, see D. Baltzer, *Ezechiel und Deuterojesaja* (Berlin: Walter de Gruyter, 1971) 141-149. Replacing the Davidic lineage in the eyes of the prophet was another ruler anointed by Yahweh, Cyrus (Isa 45:1). Not limited to the Judahite monarchy, Deutero-Isaiah's assessments and expectations focus on the international or cosmic plane with the Persian monarch.

[25]See the commentaries and especially R. North, *The Suffering Servant in Deutero-Isaiah* (London: Oxford Univ. Press, 1948), on the problems inherent in this material.

[26]Westermann, *Isaiah,* 21; see also O. Kaiser, *Der königliche Knecht* (Göttingen: Vandenhoeck & Ruprecht, 1959), 65 and *passim,* for prophetic qualities in what Kaiser argues is essentially a royal figure.

[27]Habel, "The Call Narrative," 316 note 40.

[28]For example, Engnell and Johnson cited in Muilenburg, "The Book of Isaiah," 412.

[29]Muilenburg, "The Book of Isaiah," 413; McKenzie, *Second Isaiah,* 55.

[30]See Hanson, *The Dawn of Apocalyptic,* 32-46, for a survey of critical literature and arguments in favor of a "Trito-Isaiah."

[31]Westermann, *Isaiah,* 295-296; Hanson, 42-208. Kessler's study, though placing the collection in the first post-exilic century, does little more to suggest a precise socio-historical setting; W. Kessler, "Studien zur religiösen Situation im ersten nachexilischen Jahrhundert und zur Auslegung von Jesaja 56-66," *Wissenschaftliche Zeitschrift der Martin-Luther Universität, Halle-Wittenberg* 6 (1956) 41-45.

[32]One must admit the striking similarities in style and language between Deutero- and Trito-Isaiah. Elliger has forcefully argued that the relation between the two is rather like teacher and disciple; K. Elliger, *Deuterojesaja in seinem Verhältnis zu Tritojesaja* (Stuttgart: W. Kohlhammer, 1933). A chronological placement of Trito-Isaiah before 520 B.C. certainly strengthens such a view.

[33]So Hanson, *The Dawn of Apocalyptic.*

[34]Westermann, *Isaiah,* 299.

[35]Muilenburg, "The Book of Isaiah," 717.

[36]Cf. Hanson, *The Dawn of Apocalyptic,* 53.

[37]For example, Muilenburg "The Book of Isaiah," 709; Westermann, *Isaiah,* 366; Kessler, "Studien zur religiösen Situation," 54-55.

[38]W. Cannon, "Isaiah 61:1-3 as Ebed-Yahweh Poem," *ZAW* 6 (1926) 287. Cf. Hanson, *The Dawn of Apocalyptic,* 65-67.

[39]S. Mowinckel, "The 'Spirit' and the 'Word' in the Pre-Exilic Reforming Prophets," *JBL* 53 (1954) 195-227.

[40]*lāśûm laʾăbēlê ṣiyyôn* might be secondary; Hanson, *The Dawn of Apocalyptic,* 57; Muilenburg, "The Book of Isaiah," 711. The specificity of this supposed gloss does, however, fit well with the rest of the verse.

[41]Muilenburg, "The Book of Isaiah," 709.

[42]W. Zimmerli, "Zur Sprache Tritojesaja's," *Schweizerische Theologische Umschau* 20 (1950) 110-122.

[43]Hanson hints at this explanation, ". . . the material in 55-66 was so intimately related to Second Isaiah, often assuming the form of a *pešer* on that corpus. . . ,"*Studies,* 33.

[44]D. Michel, "Zur Eigenart Tritojesajas," *Theologia Viatorum* 10 (1965-1966) 217ff.

[45]Plöger, *Theocracy and Eschatology,* 110.

[46]Michel, "Zur Eigenart Tritojesajas," 230.

[47]Hanson, *The Dawn of Apocalyptic,* 79-202.

[48]Plöger, *Theocracy and Eschatology,* 77-78.

[49]Cf. the preceding collection concerning the royal house, Jer 21:11-23:8.

[50]So also, A. Weiser, *Das Buch des Propheten Jeremia* (ATD 20/21; Göttingen: Vandenhoeck & Ruprecht, 1960-1966) 211; W. Rudolph, *Jeremia* (HAT I, 12; Tübingen: J. C. B. Mohr, 1968) 155; P. Volz, *Der Prophet Jeremia* (KAT 10; Leipzig: A. Deichertsche Buchhandlung; 1928) 245.

[51]For a review of the research on *maśśā*, see conveniently, M. Saebo, "Exkursus: Der Begriff *maśśā* als Überschrift und Fachwort in den Prophetenbüchern," *Sacharja 9-14. Untersuchungen von Text und Form* (WMANT 34; Neukirchen-Vluyn: Neukirchener Verlag, 1969) 137-140, and S. Erlandsson, *The Burden of Babylon, A Study of Isaiah 13:2-14:23.* (Coniectanea Biblica, Old Testament Series #4) Lund: Gleerup, 1970, 64ff.

[52]Reading with LXX *hymeis, ᵓattem hammaśśā*.

[53]Vs. 36b is missing in LXX[B-S, A].

[54]LXX[B-S, A] represents a shorter text in vs. 37, *kai ti elalēse kyrios ho theos hēmōn* or *ûmāh dibbēr yhwh ᵓᵉlōhênû* which is identical with the last clause of vs. 37 if *ᵓᵉlōhênû* is omitted.

[55]Missing in LXX[B, A].

[56]*nāśōᵓ* is possibly an Aramaic spelling of BH *nasoh,* but the syntax still remains difficult; perhaps *nāśōᵓ* with LXX α´, σ´; S; V. Cf. J. Janzen, *Studies in the Text of Jeremiah* (HSM 6; Cambridge: Harvard, 1973) 99. See also GK 75qq for the typical III/*he* and III/*aleph* confusion.

[57]Omit *ᵓetkem* as a gloss.

[58]Omit *mēᶜal pānâ* with LXX[B-S, A].

[59]So J. Bright, "This nucleus [vs. 33] has, however, been expanded (in vss. 34-40) by an extended commentary which is rather diffuse and not altogether to the point," *Jeremiah* (AB 21; Garden City: Doubleday, 1965) 154; or A. Weiser, "the piece does not constitute a unity," *Das Buch des Propheten Jeremia.* 211, "what follows now (vss. 34-40) lies on another plane and breathes another spirit," 212. Bright is quite correct that vss. 34-40 are not to the original point of the wordplay. Vss. 34-40 are, however, quite to the point which they intend to address, prohibiting future prophetic performance. Volz's evaluation is perhaps the most radical,"Der Abschnitt ist an sich völlig wertlos, grobstes Missverständnis . . ." *Der Prophet Jeremia* 245.

[60]See E. Nicholson, *Preaching to the Exiles* (London: Blackwell, 1970) 102-103, for the view that Jer 23:34-40 are consistent in style and tone with the rest of the collection on prophecy; cf. also Weiser, *Das Buch des Propheten Jeremia* 212.

It is, of course, possible that vss. 39-40 constitute a judgment response to the earlier condemnation in vs. 33, especially if we emend the text to read *wᵉnāśîtî* thereby continuing the use of the root *nśᵓ*. This possibility is, however, improbable because the other Jeremianic wordplay is self-contained, i.e. there is no further judgment in Jer 1:11-12.

[61]Note also Jer 23:31 which is similar in intent, but which is part of a complex which indicts the wrong sort of prophets, and not all prophetic activity.

[62]The protestations of H. Weippert against the deuteronomistic provenance of certain Jeremianic prose passages do not suggest an early date of composition for Jer 23:34-40, *Die Prosareden des Jeremiabuches* (BZAW 132; Berlin: W. de Gruyter, 1973).

[63]The deuteronomistic redactional activity surely extended over a significant span of time; cf. J. Mays on the deuteronomistic redaction of Amos, *Amos: A Commentary* (Philadelphia: Westminster, 1969) 13-14.

[64]J. Bright, "The Date of the Prose Sermons of Jeremiah," *JBL* 70 (1951) 17.

65The most recent example is E. Tov, "L'incidence de la critique textuelle sur la critique littéraire dans le livre de Jérémie," *RB* 79 (1972) 189-199.

66For other such compilations, see Nicholson, *Preaching to the Exiles* 30 n. 1 and J. Hyatt, "The Deuteronomic Edition of Jeremiah," *Vanderbilt Studies in the Humanities* I (ed. R. Beatty et al.; Nashville: Vanderbilt University, 1951) 77-78.

67Bright, "The Date of the Prose Sermons," 32-34.

68M. Weinfeld, *Deuteronomy and the Deuteronomic School* (Oxford: Clarendon, 1972) 347-348.

69Bright, "The Date of the Prose Sermons." 31.

70T. Overholt, "Remarks on the Continuity of the Jeremiah Tradition," *JBL* 91 (1972) 461.

71Nicholson, *Preaching to the Exiles,* 32-34.

72W. Thiel, *Die deuteronomistische Redaktion von Jeremia 1—25* (WMANT 41; Neukirchen-Vluyn: Neukirchener Verlag, 1973) 290-300.

73Overholt, "Remarks on the Continuity," 459-462.

74Overholt has shown that this appeal to the past was not a particularly strong argument since Isaiah had, like Hananiah, predicted the ultimate restoration of Zion, T. Overholt, "Jeremiah 27—29: the Question of False Prophecy," *JAAR* 35 (1967) 241-249.

75The contrast between Deuteronomy, chapters 13 and 18 is informative. In chapter 18 the people are not explicitly commanded to execute the prophet whereas they are so directed in chapter 13 as indicated by the purge formula, "thus you shall purge the evil from your midst." (13.6) Zech 13:2-6 (see below pp. 33ff.), in contrast, represents a nearly vigilante approach, "you shall kill the prophet."

76So Overholt, "Jeremiah 27-29;" cf. Jer 28:16; 29:21, 32.

77See Weiser, *Das Buch des Propheten Jeremia,* 212.

78*maśśāʾ* is also used to introduce other prophetic collections: Nah 1:1; Hab 1:1 and Isa 13:1.

79Hyatt, "The Deuteronomic Edition of Jeremiah," 94.

80Tov, "L'incidence de la critique textuelle," 191.

81Hyatt, "The Deuteronomic Edition of Jeremiah," 94.

82See also V. Eppstein, "The Day of Yahweh in Jer 4:23-28," *JBL* 57 (1968) 93-97, where he argues that this Jeremianic text was inserted by an early apocalyptic glossator.

83See the numerous studies by F. Cross propounding the local text theory and, more particularly, the work of his student J. Janzen, "Double Reading in the text of Jeremiah," *HTR* 60 (1967) 443-447 and *Studies in the Text of Jeremiah.*

84 Tov, "L'incidence de la critique textuelle," 198-199.

85J. Bright, "The Prophetic Reminiscence: Its Place and Function in the book of Jeremiah," *Biblical Essays,* Proceedings of the 9th Meeting of "Die ou-Testamentise Werkgemeenskap in Suid-Afrika," Univ. of Stellenbosch, July, 1966, 11-30.

86In vs. 2, MT reads *ʾaccbîr,* a reading corroborated by most LXX witnesses. However, LXX [W'ᵓ (407ᵗˣᵗ) Bo Aeth Arab] provide an option which makes sense both text-critically and in context. This LXX manuscript group reads *ekkausō,* "to burn out," instead of *exarō,* "to drive out," i.e. these texts reflect the form, *ʾabcir,* as against *ʾacabîr* in MT and most LXX manuscripts. One may easily see how a copyist mistake might have occurred. This picture of fire-produced destruction, so common to ancient Near Eastern treaty curses, fits nicely into the Zechariah threat (especially with the theme of purifying fire in vss. 7-9) and is corroborated by earlier Deuteronomic phraseology which the writer appears to have known.

Obviously, the LXX translators had problems with these two forms of *dqr.* One way to explain the difficulty in 12:10 is to hypothesize that the translator read *rdqw,* which in late Jewish script would not have been a difficult confusion. Reading *wᶜqdhw* for *wdqrhw* probably resulted in the present LXX reading in 13:3 (mistaking *d* for *ᶜ* and *r* for *d*). One can argue that the Hebrew *Vorlage* was *dqr* in both cases and that the LXX versions resulted from either scribal errors or revisions based on theological propriety. One might also contend that *ᶜqd* was the *Vorlage* in 13:3 and that the present *dqr* is secondary, a contamination from *dqr* in 12:10. I favor the MT reading as the more likely option.

[87]LXX translates with *sumpodiousin*, "to bind the feet together," so also S, *wn⁾srwnh*, see M. Saebo, *Sacharja 9-14*, 103. This is the only place that LXX has so translated *dqr, kenteō* and its various affixed forms being the normal rendition of *dqr*. Further complicating this problem is the LXX translation of the same root, *dqr*, in Zech 12:10 where LXX has *katorcheomai*, "to dance in triumph" or metaphorically, "to insult." *α΄, σ΄, θ΄* read *kai ekkentēksousin auton*, the expected translation. For a more detailed treatment of *dqr* in Zech 12:10, see M. Delcor, "Un problème du critique textuelle et d'exegèse: Zach 12:10, et aspicient ad me quem confixerunt," *RB* 58 (1951) 189ff.; J. Hoftizer, "A propos d'une interprétation recent de deux passages difficiles: Zach 12:11 et Zach 11:13," *VT* 3 (1953) 407ff.

[88]*GK* 74 and H. Mitchell, *Haggai, Zechariah, Malachi, and Jonah* (ICC; New York: Scribner's 1912) 123, explain this aberrant form as a III/*aleph* infinitive construct formed by analogy on a III/*hē* root.

[89]LXX omits the negative thereby interpreting *lᵉmaᶜan* (in Hebrew most probably a purpose clause, see R. Williams, *Hebrew Syntax, An Outline*, [Toronto: Univ. of Toronto, 1967]; #367) as a result clause. Jansma contends LXX variation results from a misreading of ⁾*adderet śēᶜār* as a "penitential garment," *derrin trichein*, cf. Isa 50:3 Rev 6:12, T. Jansma, *Inquiry into the Hebrew Text and Ancient Versions of Zechariah IX-XIV* (Leiden: Brill, 1949) 124.

[90]※ *dioti anthrōpos ergazomenos tēn gēn egō eimi* on the basis of the Hexaplaric evidence, thereby verifying the MT.

⁾*ādām hiqnanî* is extremely difficult. It may represent a hiphil of *qnh*, "a man caused me to possess." Wellhausen and Kittel suggest ⁾*dmh qnyny*, by relocating *h*, to read, "land is my possession." LXX reads *egennēse me*, "he brought me up." (We might expect *egeinēse* since *geinomai* is the more common translation for "to bring up" while *gennaō* usually means "to bear.") Various renditions of this phrase include: "taught me husbandry, made me a landowner, made me a cattleowner, sold me as a slave, bought me as a slave," Mitchell, *Haggai, Zechariah*, 340. Jerome, in defending his Latin translation, wrote, "The Syriac readings read far more simply than our Greek. For this reason, we do not think they are reconcilable with the Hebrew because if we note that Aquila and Theodotion render, for *adm, Adama* and not *anthrōpos*, then their translations are not far out of line with mine, 'since Adam has been my model from youth,'" F. Field, *Origenis Hexaplorum*, Oxford: Clarendon, 1867, 1875; reprint Hildesheim: Georg Olms, 1967, p. 1027. The Targum reads ⁾*yns⁾ ⁾qnyyny*, "one has kept me in slavery," a translation which Saebo (*Sacharja 9-14*, 104-105) considers acceptable. I favor the solution of Wellhausen and Kittel.

[91]Most LXX witnesses follow the idiomatic usage of *yādeykā* with *cheirōn*. Cf. the Ugaritic phrase in *CTA* 2.14.14, 16, *bn ydm*, "between the shoulders," and the same basic idiom in 1 Kgs 9:24. Sᶜ-V L (86ᵗˣᵗ)-407ᵐᵍ *α΄, θ΄* read *ōmōn*, "side." Mitchell thinks this reading indicates a Hebrew *Vorlage sdyk*, ". . . this being the word required by the context and the one favoured by LXX which has *ōmōs* here as well as in Isa 60:4; 66:12 where MT has *ṣd*. So also A, Σ, Θ." (*Haggai Zechariah*, 340). However, the fact that there is a North-West Semitic idiom which was correctly translated by some LXX witnesses makes Mitchell's reconstruction unnecessary.

[92]For *bēt mᵉ⁾ ahᵃbāy*, the majority of LXX witnesses read *en tō oikō tō agapētō mou*, "in my beloved house" instead of MT "house of my friends." LXX A'-544 *L* 91 CoArm Cyr.ᶠ Tht. ᴾHi. read *tou agapētou*, "house of my lover."

Otzen wants to push *mᵉ⁾ ahᵃbāy* beyond "my friends" by arguing that there is a close parallel to Jer 5:7 *bēt zōnāh*, cult prostitution. According to Otzen, *mᵉ⁾ahᵃbāy* ". . . may have become a technical designation of the deity comparable to ⁾*dny*," B. Otzen, *Studien über Deuterosacharja* (Copenhagen: Munksgaard, 1964) 197. He also adduces May's study on the fertility cult in which May wants to interpret *m⁾hb* as a name for the sacred male prostitute, an assertion which he attempts to establish on the basis of the Proto-Sinaitic inscriptions. May himself recognizes that the phrase in the inscriptions ". . . does not, of course, necessarily refer to sacred prostitution," H. May, "The Fertility Cult in Hosea," *AJSL* 48 (1931) 90 n. 3. A brief look at the inscriptions shows that the phrase actually appears only once, in #345, in unreconstructed form, W. Albright, *The Proto-Sinaitic Inscriptions* (Cambridge: Harvard, 1969) 19. If we accept Albright's translation, "Swear to give a sacrifice" and "in order that we may sacrifice to Baalath," the reference is certainly not to male cult prostitution. Consequently, a translation without $m^{e_{\circ}}ah^abay$ as a terminus technicus for cult prostitution is to be preferred. Judges 5:31 $w^{e_{\circ}}\bar{o}h^a$-$b\bar{a}yw$ suggests a more neutral meaning, "allies" or "friends."

In a private communication, S. Dean McBride has suggested that Zech 13:6 may be referring to the bacchanalian $marze^ah$ activities. (See M. Pope, "A Divine Banquet at Ugarit," *The Use of the Old Testament in the New and Other Essays*, ed. J. Efird; Durham: Duke Univ., 1972, 170ff.; and B. Porten, *Archives from Elephantine: the Life of an Ancient Jewish Military Colony*. Berkeley: Univ. of California, 1968, 179ff.) Following this hypothesis, the "prophet," embarrassed by the signs of his activity (probably ecstatic), would have attributed his stripes to a wild and orgiastic festive celebration.

[93]The debate over whether this phrase is an expression with special eschatological significance, as Gressmann and others have argued, or is simply a temporal adverb, as stated by P. Munch, *The Expression bajjôm hāhū*. *Is it an Eschatological terminus technicus?* (Oslo: Dybwad, 1936) is not important here, though Munch has overstated his case. Cf. Saebo, *Sacharja 9-14*, 262ff.

[94]Saebo, *Sacharja 9-14*, 266-267.

[95]On the problem of disparate and even conflicting traditions in Deutero-Zechariah, see H. Lutz, *Jahwe, Jerusalem und die Völker. Zur Vorgeschichte von Sach 12:1-8 und 14:1-5* (WMANT 27: Neukirchen-Vluyn: Neukirchener Verlag, 1968).

[96]Cf. Nah 1:14 and Zech 1:3, 4 on the $^{\circ}kryt$ sentence in late prophetic speech.

[97]C. Westermann, *Basic Forms of Prophetic Speech* (Philadelphia: Westminster, 1967) 48.

[98]On the formula and the related laws, see J. L'Hour, "Une législation criminelle dans le Deutéronome," *Bib* 44 (1963) 1-28. I am indebted to S. Dean McBride for this observation and reference.

[99]J. Fitzmyer, *The Aramaic Inscriptions of Sefire* (Rome: Pontifical Biblical Institute, 1967) 14.

[100]*Ibid.*, 20.

[101]K. Elliger, *Das Buch der zwölf kleinen Propheten* (Göttingen: Vandenhoeck & Ruprecht, 1950) 173.

[102]Saebo, *Sacharja 9-14*, 274.

[103]Whether one must accept Lamarche's thesis that vss. 2-6 are a consistent unit because of a chiastic structure (vss. 2-3: idols, suppression, punishment and vss. 4-6: punishment, suppression, idols), I am not sure. Perhaps the chiasm is in the eye of the beholder, P. Lamarche, *Zacharie IX-XIV. Structure litteraire et messianisme* (Paris: J. Gabalda, 1961) 89.

[104]I depend upon Otzen's survey of the scholarship, *Studien über Deuterosacharja*, 1911.

[105]Mitchell, *Haggai, Zechariah*, 337.

[106]Otzen, *Studien über Deuterosacharja*, 198.

[107]*Ibid.*, so also Saebo, *Sacharja 9-14*, 274.

[108]Hanson, *Studies in the Origins of Jewish Apocalyptic*, 367.

[109]Plöger, *Theocracy and Eschatology*, 105; H. W. Wolff, *Dodeka-propheten 5. Joel* (Neukirchen-Vluyn: Neukirchener Verlag, 1963) 3. Wolff contends that the entire book is post-exilic, a thesis which requires further investigation.

[110]This should be understood as a redactional clause and not a temporal designation; A. Ehrlich, *Randglossen zur hebräischen Bibel* (Hildesheim: Georg Olms, 1968) Vol 5, 222.

[111]Acts 2:17 reads "from my spirit." The LXX and Acts 2: 17-21 readings should, however, not be considered as evidence of an earlier variant text.

[112]Following Wolff who reads the piel denominatively here, *Joel*, 65.

[113]For this meaning of w^egam, cf. Gen 19:22; 27:34.

[114]$tîm^arôt$ is difficult. The usual explanation is to cite the root *tmr*, "date palm," and suggest that the form in Joel refers to a cloud of similar shape, i.e. a volcanic cloud. Cf. the same phrase in Cant 3:6 where it is also plural; Wolff, *Joel*, 66; W. Rudolph, *Joel-Amos-Obadja-Jona* (Gutersloh: Gerd Mohn, 1971), 70; T. H. Robinson, *Die zwölf kleinen Propheten. Hosea bis Micha* (Tübingen: J. C. B. Mohr, 1954) 66.

[115] qr°. . . b is an idiom used to denote an intensive relationship, Wolff, *Joel,* 66.

[116] $\hat{u}ba\check{s}\check{s}^e r\hat{\imath}d\hat{\imath}m$ is unclear. It is probably secondary, following the concluding formula $ka^{\circ a}\check{s}er$ $^{\circ}\bar{a}mar\ yhwh$. There have been a good many proposals to explain its meaning: Ehrlich, "the angel of death;" Jerome, "an obscure place name." My solution is to omit b on the basis of vertical dittography and to read "survivors." The point of the gloss seems to be the contrast between certain individuals calling on Yahweh, vs. 5a, and the necessity for the survivors to be called by Yahweh, vs. 5c.

[117] Plöger, *Theocracy and Eschatology,* 101ff.

[118] Rudolph, *Joel,* 69ff.

[119] Wolff, *Joel,* 67-68.

[120] *Ibid.,* 9-12.

[121] Rudolph, *Joel,* 69.

[122] Wolff, *Joel,* 78.

[123] Cf. Munch, The Expression $bajj\hat{o}m\ h\bar{a}h\hat{u}^{\circ}$, *passim.*

[124] G. von Rad, "The Origin of the Day of the Lord," *JSS* 4 (1959) 97-108. F. Cross has argued that the Day of Yahweh is the culmination of the cosmic battle, a day of victory and a celebration of Yahweh's kingship; "The Divine Warrior in Israel's Early Cult," *Biblical Motifs: Origins and Transformations* (Cambridge: Harvard Univ. Press, 1966) 24ff., and *CMHE* 94-111. Of these two tradition elements, the martial activity would seem to be primary for the biblical day of Yahweh traditions. Cf. Wolff, *Joel* 38-39.

[125] The spirit poured out from on high (Isa 32:15), a fructifying force, is an earlier stage in the spirit-pouring tradition.

[126] Cf. Rudolph, *Joel,* 72, where he argues that the Ezekiel and Zechariah texts present the spirit being poured out in the End-time whereas in Joel it is preliminary to the eschaton.

[127] Note also Ezek 36:27; 37:14 for Yahweh's placing his spirit within the true Yahwist.

[128] Rudolph, *Joel,* 72 note 6, who cites P. Volz, *Der Geist Gottes,* 110, 92ff.

[129] Wolff, *Joel,* 79.

[130] A. Kapelrud, *Joel Studies* (Uppsala: Almquist & Wiksells, 1948), 141.

[131] Jeremias, *Theophanie,* 98ff.

[132] Wolff, *Joel,* 81.

[133] Heiler, *Erscheinungsformen und Wesen der Religion,* 56. The reference to the copper color of the lunar eclipse which Robinson proposes is reductionistic, Robinson, *Die zwölf kleinen Propheten,* 67.

[134] On Zion as *Rettungsort* and *Fluchtberg,* see Wolff, *Joel,* 81-82. Also note the tradition of the nations against Jerusalem and Zion discussed by Lutz, *Jahwe, Jerusalem und die Völker.*

[135] Wolff, *Joel,* 81.

[136] See Wolff's discussion of the two day of Yahweh traditions, *Joel,* 38-39.

[137] On the older covenantal formula, "I will be your God and you shall be my people," (Exod 6:7) upon which the Joel and Zechariah idioms apparently draw, see Weinfeld, *Deuteronomy and the Deuteronomic School,* 80-81, and N. Lohfink, "Dt 26, 17-19 und die 'Bundesformel,'" *ZKT* 91 (1969) 517-553.

[138] Holladay's observation is most enlightening, "Although the term $mal^{\circ}\bar{a}k$, 'messenger,' only rarely appears in the books of the pre-exilic prophets, and never . . . with the intended meaning 'heavenly messenger,' it is hardly a chance matter that the last prophet in the Hebrew canon styled himself (or was named) Malachi, 'my messenger;'" Holladay, "Assyrian Statecraft and the Prophets of Israel," 30-31.

[139] This is not to say that the more general expectation of prophecy did not continue as a viable option in its own right. See the use of Joel 3 in Acts 2.

[140] This implied criticism of the Levites in a late deutero-prophetic collection provides an informative contrast to the pro-Levitical bias in Chronicles, cf. also Mal 2:8.

[141] R. Pfeiffer, "Die Disputationsworte im Buche Malachi," *EvTh* 19 (1959) 546ff.

[142] Note the Deuteronomistic stamp of the admonitions in Mal 3:5 (cf. Deut 18:10 to the legal material in the book of the Covenant).

[143]Eissfeldt, *The Old Testament*, 442.

[144]Against Robinson, *Die zwölf kleinen Propheten*, 275; Sellin, *Das Zwölfprophetenbuch*, 617; who emphasizes the ethical demands; and those who see here evidence of disruption of Jewish family life by Hellenistic culture.

Chapter III

Chronicles and Levitical Prophets

A. Chronicles and Levitical Singers

So far, we have examined the character of prophecy in the deutero-prophetic collections and have attempted to delineate the nature of the development from a prophetic office, which apparently ceased with the end of the Davidic line, to certain traditions about prophecy which became a part of the *praeparatio* in the eschatological scenario.

There is, however, another side to the coin. The deutero-prophetic writers were not the only members of the post-exilic Israelite community reflecting about prophecy and making claims about the proper use and authority of classical prophetic formulae, titles and literature. Failure to recognize the importance of prophecy in Chronicles has created the illusion of a unilinear development from prophecy to apocalyptic. Plöger, Hanson, and North, among others, have been intent on demonstrating certain continuities between the classical prophetic literature and apocalyptic texts like Daniel. But by exclusively emphasizing this development and by ignoring the presence of prophetic claims in the hierocratic group, a group posited as the opposition to the deutero-prophetic writers, the picture of post-exilic prophetic traditions has become one-sided.

Prophetic traditions are of profound importance to the Chronicler's work. Prophecy was the mode by which the monarchy was founded, informed and ultimately destroyed.[1] In I Chr: 11:3, we learn that David was made king "according to the word of the Lord by Samuel." The Chronicler also evaluated the monarchy's fate on the basis of Israel's response to the prophets:

> The Lord, the God of their fathers, sent persistently to them by his messengers, because he had compassion on his people and on his dwelling place; but they kept mocking the messengers of God, despising his words, and scoffing at his prophets, till the wrath of the Lord rose against his people, till there was no remedy. (2 Chr 36:15-16)

The dogma for Israelite success was also closely connected with the prophets:

> Hear me, Judah and the inhabitants of Jerusalem. Believe in the Lord your God, and you will be established; believe his prophets and you will succeed. (2 Chr 20:20)

The long succession of prophets who accompanied Israel's kings further testifies to the significance of prophecy for the Chronicler.[2] Prophecy was the primary mode of divine communication to the Davidic state. Hence to suggest that Chronicles, as part of the hierocracy, is anti-prophetic or that Chronicles is a work in which prophetic traditions are insignificant, is a serious misunderstanding of the text.

From the perspective of the so-called Chronicler's history,[3] prophecy did not cease with the end of the nation, since Ezra 5—6 depicts the prophets Haggai and Zechariah in pivotal roles. Innumerable commentators have observed the centrality of the temple for the Chronicler; and it is with the reconstruction of the temple that the Chronicler records the end of classical prophetic activity. The account of Haggai and Zechariah's work surrounds the missives of Tattenai and Darius. Work on the temple had stopped when Artaxerxes was advised that Jerusalem was a troublesome city. Then, without receiving any dispensation from their overlords, the citizens of Jerusalem and Judah, under impetus from the prophets, began to work again on the temple:

> Now the prophets, Haggai and Zechariah the son of Iddo, prophesied to the Jews who were in Judah and Jerusalem, in the name of the God of Israel who was over them. Then Zerubbabel the son of Shealtiel and Jeshua the son of Jozadak arose and began to rebuild the house of God which was in Jerusalem; and with them were the prophets of God, helping them. (Ezra 5:1-2)

After the Tattenai and Darius exchange, the account continues: "The elders built and prospered, through the prophesying of Haggai the prophet and Zechariah the son of Iddo" (Ezra 6:14).

The remarkable feature of these two chapters in Ezra is the contrast they present to the accounts in the prophetic books. In the books of Haggai and Zechariah, the prophets work for the reinstitution of the monarchy as well as the reconstruction of the temple. In the Chronistic history, they are responsible only for temple reconstruction. Their rhetoric in support of Zerubbabel plays no role in the Chronistic history. This contrast can not be overestimated, especially because of the Chronicler's proclivity to juxtapose prophets with royal figures. Attempts to crown Zerubbabel were unacceptable to the Chronicler's view of the post-exilic communities' political needs.[4] Reinstitution of the monarchy was needless since David, the sufficient monarch, had already given Israel the temple. With proper prophetic aid, the temple was to serve as the sole focal point of the new community, a theocracy in which Yahweh's rule was manifest.

Consistent with a lack of interest in monarchy as the mode of governance in the second temple period, there is scant evidence to suggest the Chronicler awaited the appearance of a Davidic heir or the return of prophecy.[5] Instead there is a form of realized eschatology. Just as the Davidic ideal is bound up with the reconstructed temple, so prophecy is, it appears, tied to the work of certain temple personnel, the Levitical singers. Since the group of which the Chronistic writers were a part had a consistently worked-out view of prophecy, it is no wonder that the deutero-prophetic writers took a polemical stance when considering prophecy in their own time.

Assuming a basic dichotomy of outlooks on prophecy in the post-exilic period, it is therefore necessary to examine the literature written by those who have been characterized as the "theocracy," "those in power," "the hierocracy," or "the non-eschatological group." The rationale for choosing Chronicles to represent this perspective is virtually self-evident. As both Rudolph and Plöger have said, "The Chronicler seeks to portray the realization of theocracy on the soil of Israel,"[6] an ideology which directly opposes the expectations of the deutero-prophetic writers as expressed in the eschatological scenario.

In order to study a counterpoise to the deutero-prophetic texts, I shall examine several passages within the Chronicler's work, texts which use the various appellations for prophet, *nābî*, *ḥōzeh*, *rōʾeh*, to designate members of Levitic groups. Though there are only five such texts (I Chronicles 25; 2 Chronicles 20; 29; 34:30; and 35:15), and of these only three demand extensive study, these passages have signal importance since the Chronicler is here using prophetic titles to describe one of his favorite themes, the function and importance of the Levites. These texts present valuable sources for discovering the way in which a non-deutero-prophetic, post-exilic writer understood prophetic authority and prophetic performance in his own time.[7]

Before beginning with the specific texts dealing with Levitical prophets, two topics require brief discussion. First, there is the matter of date and redaction of Chronicles. This is no simple topic because the question of date of composition, redaction, and the relationship between Chronicles and Ezra-Nehemiah are inextricably related. I make no claim to have solved these issues, and yet it is important to make clear one's position on these matters—the more so since consensus on these topics is as uncertain now as perhaps any time in this century.

The primary reason for uncertainty in dating the Chronicler's history lies in the complex redactional development which the narrative has undergone. Does one assign the date of composition to the earliest version of Chronicles or does one assign it to the final, redacted product? Some would argue, as Galling does, that the basic history was written at the end of the Persian period and that this composition was edited about a century later.[8] Myers makes no such distinctions and opts for a date of c. 400 B.C.[9] Furthermore, the decision of whether or not to include Ezra-Nehemiah as a part of the Chronicler's history places immediate limits on decisions about date. If these books are to be included, then the Chronicler cannot predate Nehemiah. If not, then the Chronicler's history might have been written significantly earlier than the date of Nehemiah.

The question whether Chronicles and Ezra-Nehemiah comprise one work must be addressed first. Sara Japhet has conveniently listed the four major points adduced in the argument that the Chronicler's work includes Ezra-Nehemiah:

1. The presence of the first verses of Ezra at the end of Chronicles.
2. 1 Esdras begins with 2 Chr 35—36 and continues through Ezra.
3. The linguistic resemblance between the books is revealed by common vocabulary, syntactic phenomena, and stylistic peculiarities.
4. The alleged uniformity of theological conceptions, expressed both in the material and its selection.[10]

Japhet, however, argues convincingly that Chronicles is so different in style and vocabulary from Ezra-Nehemiah that we must conclude these works stem from two authors in different historical periods. Furthermore, Freedman's and Willi's analyses of the theological methodologies and interests strongly suggest that two different perspectives are at work, that of the Chronicler and that of the author of Ezra-Nehemiah.[11] As for the overlapping verses, I follow Freedman's cogent suggestion:

> It seems to me that the repetition of the verses is a late phenomenon and the result of the division and ordering of the books in the Massoretic text, and has no immediate bearing on the question (of common authorship).[12]

The same basic argument may be made for the overlap in 1 Esdras. Hence it is probable that Chroniclers and Ezra-Nehemiah represent two separate works.

If Chronicles may be viewed as independent from Ezra-Nehemiah, what is the date of its composition? Following Freedman, I suggest that the basic work of the Chronicler, to be distinguished from work of later redactors, was produced c. 500 B.C. If, as Rudolph, Freedman, and Plöger have all argued, the Chronicler functions essentially as a legitimist for the post-exilic cultic community, then we should expect such charter activity at the time when the temple cult was being revived, viz. in the decades following the rededication of the temple in c. 515 B.C.[13]

Bickerman has directed two arguments against dating Chronicles in the sixth or fifth centuries. First he contends that the Chronicler's historiographic method depends upon or shares the method of the fifth-century Greek historian, Herodotus. However, this assertion depends upon rather broad characterizations of Chronicles: "his purpose is not to give a mere chronicle but to provide a clue to the meaning and direction of Israel's history,"[14] "he stresses the idea of personal responsibility," "the Chronicler describes the whole of human history from his standpoint." All these characteristics would also obtain for a sixth-century Israelite narrative, the deuteronomistic history, which most certainly does not depend upon Herodotus' method.

Second, Bickerman's attempts to distinguish the deuteronomistic historiography from that of the Chronicler are forced.[15] For example, he argues that the Chronicler differs from the deuteronomistic writer in his assessment of personal responsibility. The Chronicler records Manasseh being punished for his own sins (2 Chr 33:11) whereas in 2 Kgs 24:3 the deuteronomistic historian understands the fate of Jehoiakim (not the captivity of Jehoiachin as Bickerman asserts, p. 25) to be the punishment for the sins of Manasseh. Rather than espousing a general theory of personal retribution, the Chronicler is most probably preserving an independent tradition about Manasseh.[16] So too Bickerman wants to distinguish between the Chronicler's and the deuteronomistic writer's views of Joash's defeats. However, 2 Chr 24:24 (supposedly representing the view of individual retribution) reads "because they had forsaken the Lord, the God of their fathers," whereas 2 Kgs 17:7 (supposedly characterizing the view of corporate retribution) states "and this was so because the people of Israel had sinned against the Lord." There is no essential distinction between these two perspectives. Hence it is improper to argue that Chronicles is late because it presents an historiography significantly different from that of the deuteronomistic history.

A second recent critic of an early dating for Chronicles, P. Welten, understands the history of the late post-exilic period to be reflected in the Chronicler's history. To be more precise, Welten argues that in three *Topoi*, war reports, descriptions of military techniques, and reports about buildings and fortifications, the Chronicler portrays the conditions of his own time. Welten's investigation of these three *Topoi* however does not automatically lead to a specific dating for the book; hence discussion of date is reserved for *Exkurs* #3.[17] In that note, he rather arbitrarily states that the earliest date for the Chronicler's history is c. 400 B.C. and that a time of composition between 400 and 200 is to be expected. Since Welten argues that battle descriptions in Chronicles are strongly influenced by Greek martial techniques, he concludes that the Chronicler probably wrote in the first half of the third century B.C.

The arguments of Welten make it difficult to contend that all of Chronicles was written before the early part of the fifth century, but his theory that the book essentially represents the unsettled conditions in Judah at the time of conflict between the Ptolemies and the Seleucids remains an hypothesis. Although Welten's monograph is an extremely valuable commentary on the post-exilic period and Greek influence in that time, influence which predated Alexander, his analysis leaves open the question of the date of the Chronicler's basic history.

As for the nature of the redaction of the Chronicler's basic history written c. 500, there is likewise no consensus. The Chronicler's work has been explained in basically three ways. Some scholars have been satisfied to see the books as free from systematic redaction and basically the product of one hand. Myers' *Anchor Bible* commentary is a recent exposition of this viewpoint.[18] Most critics who adopt this stance recognize that there are additions and revisions in the text, but attempts to explain or identify these instances are usually not made. A mediating position has been taken by some like Galling, who, noting redactional activity, proposes two basic authors: "the Chronicler" who wrote the basic document in the last decades of the Persian period, and "the Chronicler**" who was responsible for the total work: Chronicles through Nehemiah.[19] A more nuanced position growing out of the work of Rothstein and Hänel's commentary identifies a plethora of redactional activity. Rothstein argued that at least four identifiable hands were observable in 1 Chronicles with two dominant strands, as well as other additions. While no one today is willing to proceed with the certainty of Rothstein in distinguishing the "Chronicler's redactor" from the "younger Chronicler's redactor," many have found his source critical arguments compelling. Welch's *The Work of the Chronicler* follows in this tradition, as does the commentary of Rudolph. Rudolph simply states that a number of late additions from more than one hand and period are discernible, but systematic identification of these hands is virtually impossible.[20] Most recently, Cross has argued for three basic editions in Chronicles-Nehemiah:

Chr_1 (c. 520 B.C.) 1 Chr 10—2 Chr 34 + 1 Esdras 1:1—5:65
Chr_2 (c. 450 B.C.) 1 Chr 10—2 Chr 34 + *Vorlage* of 1 Esdras
Chr_3 (c. 400 B.C.) 1 Chr 1—9 + 1 Chr 10—2 Chr 36:23 + Hebrew Ezra-
        Nehemiah.[21]

For this scheme to be acceptable, one must allow that Chr_2 and Chr_3 involved some redactional activity within the earliest Chronicler's work, 1 Chr 10-2 Chr 34, as well as the more obvious development by accretion. Hence I find myself in basic agreement with Cross' position as long as it includes provision for internal as well as additive redaction.

A second matter for preliminary consideration is the problem of the Levitical singers, because they appear to be described by the use of prophetic titles and nomenclature. Furthermore, there can be little doubt that the Chronicler was especially interested in the Levites (1 Chr 9:23; 2 Chr 35).[22] Furthermore, among the Levites, one small sub-group receives major attention. Köberle's monograph drew attention to the special nature of this singer group as a significant post-exilic development in some way related to the Korahite traditions. Köberle argued that the predecessor of this group was connected to the pre-exilic temple functionaries, door-keepers and singers.[23]

However, Köberle's study did little more than focus attention on this topic. Later, von Rad, in treating the Chronicler's history, devoted part of a chapter to the Levitical singers. He showed that interest in them was directly related to ark traditions (e.g. 1 Chronicles 15, a perspective not unlike that depicted in Deut 10:8; 18:5). Von Rad said: "The post-exilic Levitical movement appealed to their ark tradition in obvious opposition to the priestly-Aaronite tabernacle because the ark was given over exclusively to Levitic protection."[24] When the ark was taken into the temple, the Levites were given a new task, the temple song (1 Chr 6:16) because their work with the ark had ended.

Von Rad's second major contribution was to note that the description of the singer activity was not homogeneous and to argue that two phases of Levitical activity are presented in Chronicles. The first phase merely distinguishes specializations in cultic function: Levites as singers and as door-keepers,[25] whereas the second stage presents singing as the more important of the Levitic functions, at least in the tradition buttressed by the ark and

Davidic authorizations.

A third area of von Rad's analysis deals with distinctions within the singer groups. He makes several significant observations. (1) In Ezra-Nehemiah, the familial trinity of Asaph, Heman, Ethan/Jeduthun is not present; only Asaph is named. (2) There is no connection between the singers and the ark in the early stages of singer traditions. (3) The first Chronicler was unaware of the threefold family division. (4) The name "Jeduthun" is probably an artificial formation (later replaced by Ethan). (5) The name change from "Jeduthun" to "Ethan" correlates with the change in Levitical service, from ark carrier to singer. (6) Rothstein went too far in seeing rivalries between Levitic families. Instead of assuming intra-Levitical strife, von Rad theorized a simple case of Hemanite ascendancy and a consequent de-emphasis on other parties.[26] Though most of these observations were cogent and have been accepted by later scholarship, von Rad was unable to make sense of the heterogeneity in singer traditions: why there were two and then three divisions, and how the variations developed.

Gese's article completed the traditio-historical work on the cultic singer traditions in the second-temple period.[27] Gese was able to demonstrate four stages of development. The earliest (I) was preserved in Ezra 2 and Neh 7, lists of those who returned from exile. At this point the singers are not called Levites and are only spoken of as the sons of Asaph. A second stage (II) is represented by Neh 11:3-19 and 1 Chr 9:1b-18. Here we find the singers called Levites (still in opposition to the door-keepers) and derived from two progenitors: Asaph and Jeduthun. Moving from the Chronicler's sources to the Chronicler himself, we approach stage IIIA, where the Levitical singers are now three strong: Asaph, Heman, and Jeduthun (1 Chr 16:4; 2 Chr 5:12; 2 Chr 29:13ff.; 2 Chr 35:15), with Asaph receiving primary attention. However, with stage IIIB (1 Chr 6:16-32; 15:16-24; 16:4-42), we note more than just a change in names, i.e. Ethan replaced Jeduthan. For now Heman receives the lion's share of interest while Asaph fades into the background. Gese notes that those passages assigned to IIIB occur in what can be assessed as secondary passages.[28]

Gese claims this stratification of tradition informs us about actual groups of singers in post-exilic Israel. It seems that in the fifth century, a second group of singers, called Jeduthun, appeared alongside the Asaph group, an originally non-Levitic group who were apparently singers in the pre-exilic period. This Jeduthun, included among the Levites on the basis of an artificial name and loose genealogical derivation, was not comprised of a returning singer group from Babylon, but apparently developed in Palestine. The origins of the Hemanite group are, in all probability, to be seen as a part of the artificial construct—the Jeduthun group—and yet distinguished within the Jeduthun construct from the very beginning.

With reference to 2 Chr 20, which speaks only of an Asaph and a Korah group, Gese concludes that the Jeduthun group is implied when the Korah group is mentioned since Jeduthun is the name used when only two singer groups are present, Asaph of course being the other. Ergo, the Korah group and at least part of the Jeduthun group are similar if not identical. Gese concludes that the Chronicler designated the non-Asaphite singers, Heman and Jeduthun, as descendants of Korah. In short, the story of the second-temple Levitical singers reveals the ascendancy of the Korahites at the expense of the pre-exilic Asaphite singer group, neither of which groups were originally Levites.[29] Genealogical variations reflect the changing status of certain singer groups within the post-exilic cult.

I find this explanation of the Levitical singers' traditions very illuminating and intend to utilize it to pursue a question central to this study—how are the prophetic titles and references in these singer traditions to be understood? It should be stated at the outset that for many critics, this question has already been answered. Both von Rad and Gese assert that the prophetic material used to describe the post-exilic singers is a carry-over from pre-exilic cultic prophecy of which these second-temple singers are a remnant.[30] However, since our knowledge about pre-exilic cultic prophecy is so uncertain, assertions about continuity between this phenomenon and the Levitical singers are not very helpful. Furthermore, the case for pre-exilic cultic prophecy upon which Gese and von Rad depend is not without its own problems. The definitive statement of the cultic prophecy thesis *vis-à-vis* Levitical singers is Mowinckel's *Kultprophetie und prophetische Psalmen*.[31] Before briefly sketching Mowinckel's argument, let me say that this move of von Rad and Gese is natural in a way, but odd in light of the tradition-history evidence. It will become apparent that the prophetic terminology was used only in the latest stages of the singer traditions. Rather than being a residue or carry-over from the pre-exilic period, the prophetic appellations appear to be an innovation on the part of the Chronicler and his compatriots. This fact in itself should restrain the immediate appeal to cult prophecy as a way of understanding the Levitical singers.

The third part of Mowinckel's *Psalmenstudien* attempts to show the place of the prophetic element in Israel's cult. Since I have considered the more general questions about classical Israelite prophecy earlier, I want to examine here Mowinckel's specific treatment of Chronicles.[32] 1 Chr 15:22 and 27 are the keystone verses to his argument. According to Mowinckel, this chapter demonstrates the existence of cult prophecy at the Solomonic temple. His thesis rests on the word *bammaśśāʾ* which Mowinckel takes to mean "oracle," thereby justifying the claim that the passage is about prophecy. The authority of a Levite, a cultic official, over a prophetic element, the oracle, serves to demonstrate the existence of pre-exilic cultic prophecy for Mowinckel. This argument, however, runs counter to Mowinckel's other uses of the Chronicler's history.[33] In other places, he cites Chronicles to describe the nature of cultic prophecy in the second-temple period. Yet here he assumes 1 Chronicles 15 to be a description of the pre-exilic cult, and the grounds for accepting this chapter as an accurate description of Davidic times are not given.

Furthermore, the passage which Mowinckel has cited as the basis for his thesis is open to more than one interpretation. In 1 Chronicles 15, the Chronicler is describing the bringing-up of the ark to Jerusalem, an event of signal importance for the Chronicler, as von Rad has shown. In this context (vss. 16-24) we are presented with a description of Levitical classifications and more specifically with the divisions of the musicians' duties. In vs. 22, Chenaniah is described and charged with the following statement, *śar halwiyyim yāśōr bammaśśāᵓ kî mēbîn hûᵓ*.[34] There are three possible translations for *maśśāᵓ* within this verse. (1) *maśśāᵓ* can mean "a bearing or carrying."[35] Since 2 Chr 35:3 uses this same word to describe the Levites carrying the ark, this meaning is a valid option. The translation would then be, "Chenaniah, leader of the Levites in carrying, shall be in charge of carrying because he is expert at it," i.e. in the proper method of carrying the ark. (2) A second option is to derive a meaning from the root *nsᵓ*, "to lift up the voice or sing" (cf. Rudolph's *anstimmen*). The RSV chooses this option by translating, "Chenaniah, leader of the Levites in music, should direct the music, because he understood it." (3) A final possibility accepts Mowinckel's use of the meaning "oracle," also found in 2 Chr 24:27 and in Jer 23:34ff. as we have seen, "Chenaniah, leader of the Levites in oracles, since he was skillful at the art of giving oracles."

Rothstein argues that MT was originally *wśr* > *yśr* and then under Aramaic influence became *ysr, yśr* deriving from the denominative *śyr*, as in V and T: "He was the greatest." He further suggests that we omit the first *bammaśśāᵓ* with LXX as well as the *śar halwiyyim*, leaving an original description of Chenaniah as "head of the *bammaśśāᵓ* because he was an expert." The only textual evidence to which Mowinckel can appeal for support is the Vulgate *prophetiae praeerat*. And this is almost surely, as Rothstein has argued, a further paraphrase of the ambiguous MT.

Rothstein is correct, I think in arguing that since the controlling theme in the chapter is the carrying of the ark,[36] we should see this same concern reflected in the word *maśśāᵓ*: Chenaniah is chief of those in charge of carrying the ark. Again I refer to von Rad's demonstration that the Levitical office and the ark are themes central to the Chronicler.[37] Since Rothstein does not want to exclude the musical allusion which has been emphasized in the LXX versions, perhaps we should infer some sort of *double entendre* in the text.

Vs. 27 presents a similar problem, though here the theme of song is more explicit. The clause is: *haśśar hammaśśāᵓ hamśōrᵉrîm*. Most have translated it, "Chenaniah the leader of the music of the singers" (so also the RSV in changing *hammaśśāᵓ* to *bammaśśāᵓ* as in vs. 22). Mowinckel's decision to render *maśśāᵓ* as oracle creates some difficulty in translation. Perhaps he would read: "the leader of the oracles of the singers." LXX reads, "and Chonein the leader of songs." The Hebrew syntax is considerably less clear than the Greek.[38] Following most scholars, a translation of vs. 27 which maintains thematic continuity, i.e. leader of the music of the singers, seems more acceptable than the rendition proposed by Mowinckel.

In light of the difficulties presented by 1 Chr 15:22 and 27 and the concomitant improbability of Mowinckel's translations, his assertions about the existence of a group of pre-exilic cultic singer prophets seem tenuous. Hence one must enter a *caveat* against von Rad's and Gese's acceptance of Mowinckel's argument as a way of understanding Chronicles texts which describe Levitical singers.

I now propose to investigate the Chronicler's assessment of the Levitical singers as prophets by examining five texts. In this study, I hope to analyze texts roughly contemporaneous with those examined in the last chapter, thereby gaining a counterpoise to the deutero-prophetic view of prophecy.

B. Heman, the King's Seer

1 Chronicles 25 stands as a monument to numerous theories about the Levitic functions and prophecy. Prophecy with musical instruments, as well as the description of Heman the singer, as the king's seer, are not items susceptible to simple explanation. In tandem with forbidding genealogical lists, these unusual themes create a puzzling combination of material. Nonetheless this segment of the Chronicler's work is of critical importance for what it reveals about those who made claims for Levitical singers as prophets and about the Chronicler's view of post-exilic prophetic performance.

1 Chronicles 25:

1 David and the cultic leaders[39] designated[40] for service the sons of Asaph, Heman, and Jeduthun, who were to prophesy[41]with zithers, harps, and cymbals. The number of men so commissioned with respect to their service was:
2 Of the sons of Asaph: Zaccur, Joseph, Nethaniah and Asharelah; the sons of Asaph were under the authority of Asaph who prophesied under the authority of the king.
3 Of Jeduthun, the sons of Jeduthun: Gedaliah, Zeri, Jeshaiah,[42] Hashabiah, and Mattithiah; six, under the authority of their father Jeduthun, who prophesied with the harp for the thanksgiving and praise of Yahweh.
4 Of Heman, the sons of Heman: Bukkiah, Mattaniah, Uzziel, Shebuel, and Jerimoth, Hananiah, Hanani, Eliathah, Giddalti, Romamti-Ezer, Joshbekashah, Mallothi, Hothir, Mahazioth;
5 All these were the sons of Heman, the king's seer, according to the words of the Lord, to raise up his horn.[43] God gave to Heman fourteen sons and three daughters.
6 All these were under the authority of their father(s) for song, in the house of Yahweh, with cymbals, harps, and zithers—for the service of of the Lord's house[44] under the authority of the king, Asaph, Heman, and Jeduthun.
7 The number of the skilled ones, together with their brothers instructed in Yahweh's music was two hundred and eighty-eight.
8 And they cast lots for the service:
   the old as well as the young,
   the teacher as well as the student.

The most famous problem in this chapter is the series of names beginning with Hananiah in vs. 4. Early on, scholars noted that these names fell somewhat outside the normal gamut of Hebrew onomastic formations.[45] Inevitably, there were attempts to read the names as parts of a poetic composition, hymn fragment, or whatever. While the most thorough linguistic treatment has been offered by Haupt, the specific translations presented by Curtis, Rudolph, Myers, *et al.* appear to have won majority acceptance in reading the verse as a hymn fragment.[46]

An interesting, though often ignored, proposal has been offered by Torczyner.[47] Idiosyncratic and rather free with the text, he has focused on a problem depicted earlier by Rothstein: the singers occur in a different order in vs. 4 than they do in vss. 23-31. Rothstein's graphic presentation showed this very clearly.[48] Torczyner, unimpressed by earlier efforts at translating vs. 4b and evidently noting the same arrangement as that depicted by Rothstein, translated the names as a hymnic piece in the order in which the names occur in vss. 23-31. Though this effort recognizes a real problem, the lack of correspondence between vss. 2-4 and vss. 9-31, Torczyner's rendition fails to offer the linguistic arguments necessary to refute earlier work and, as mentioned earlier, requires rather drastic textual surgery.[49]

Ehrlich's words should remain as a reminder about the difficulty of these verses: "Out of the last nine names of the sons of Heman, scholars have recently made a prayer. And yet, what sort of Hebrew is the result?"[50] Nevertheless, the following rendition of the supposed Hebrew *Vorlage* hopefully does justice both to the complexities of the text and to previous exegetical work:

hnny[51] *yh hnny*	Be gracious to me, O Yahweh, Be gracious
ʾly ʾth[52]	Come my God
šgdlty[53] *wrmmty*	Whom I praise and extol
ᶜzry[54] *bqšty*[55] *mlʾh*[56]	My helper, fulfill my request
hwtyr[57] *mhzyʾt*[58]	Give abundant visions.

One of the obvious questions to be asked of this psalmette is that of the chicken or the egg. Which came first, the names or the poem? The fact that I have produced a reconstruction of the present text suggests that I think the present form was adapted from an earlier hymn and is not a freely created piece. Proving this assumption is another matter. Supposing that one could delimit a form-critical type of which the psalm fragment was a part, we could be fairly sure that the psalm fragment was primary. And one can, I think, discern one characteristic of the individual lament on the basis of the introductory use of *hnny*, cf. Pss 6:3; 31:10; 51:3.[59] However, behind this evanescent whiff, no traditional elements appear other than the appeal for help from one's foes. One may therefore suggest that the poem, an individual lament, is primary, though this conclusion must remain tentative.

Rudolph has suggested that the hymnic fragment be understood as demonstrating the same interconnection between names and cultic songs as in certain supposed Sumerian analogues, thereby demonstrating the lack of artificiality in vs. 4b.[60] However, in examining Gemser's statements we find a series of Sumerian names (e.g. *Lugal-šibir-za-gin-šu-du,* "the King rules with a lazur scepter") which Gemser says reminds one of a hymn or liturgical fragment.[61] That there were "actually Psalm quotations as real names" as Rudolph states, is never claimed by Gemser nor, so far as I am able to ascertain, by van Selms.

The apparent purpose of this poetic piece is to advance a claim of superior status for the Levitic singers by designating them as prophets. And within this nexus, the emphasis in 1 Chronicles 25 is on the Hemanite line: the raising of his horn (vs. 5). Surely this artifice in vs. 4b, the poetic piece intermeshed with the sons of Heman and the mention of visions within a chapter which is using prophetic appellations, is a striking technique—a *double entendre* by which the redactor was able to press his Levitic-prophetic and pro-Hemanite argument.[62]

Moving to another issue, the nature of the present text, we may discern several stages of growth within this chapter. The chapter as a whole does not represent an original unity. A number of observations speak for this thesis. (1) The *mispārām* which occurs in vs. 1 demands a specific number to follow it. However, we do not find this numerical complement until vs. 7. This hiatus has led many to argue that vss. 2-6 are an insertion. Curtis contends that the same stylistic element may be observed in Ezra 2:2b and Neh 7:7b where *mispārām* is used and the numerical complement does not occur until Ezra 2:64 and Neh 7:66; in opposition to Curtis' argument, it should be noted that in the list of returnees, we are dealing with something other than the Chronicler's own style.[63] Further, the dual usage of *mispārām* in 1 Chronicles 25, in vs. 1 and 7 (it only occurs once in Ezra and Nehemiah passages), is pleonastic and suggests a disrupted text. (2) The doublet beginnings in vss. 5 and 6 seem a bit odd. They could indicate a copying error, an attempt to legitimate an insertion, or a conflate text. (3) The order of the names of the three fathers and the instruments is not regular. In vs. 1, we find Asaph, Heman, and Jeduthun whereas in vss. 2-4, it is Asaph, Jeduthun, and Heman. In vs. 1, the order is harps, psalteries, cymbals whereas in vs. 6, cymbals, psalteries, and harps. (4) The inclusion of the hymnic fragment shows that the chapter is not a homogeneous creation. (5) The numerical evaluation of the progeny of the three fathers is missing in vs. 2 with Asaph. (6) The pattern of the temple service seems at best irregular. Rothstein, when charting the rotation of the singers in vss. 9-31, discovered that the composition was not symmetrical.[64] Of the twenty-four singers, Heman's group did not begin until the sixth turn—Asaph and Jeduthun had divided the first five stations. Furthermore, the hymnic names were stuck on at the end. Beginning with Hananiah, the names are exclusively Hemanite; and yet strikingly, they are not in the same order that we meet them in vs. 4:

Asaph	Jeduthun	Heman
1. Joseph	2. Gedaliah	—
3. Zaccur	4. Isri	—
5. Nataniah	—	6. Bukkiah
7. Jesharelah	8. Jeshaiah	9. Mattaniah
—	10. Shimei	11. Azarel
—	12. Hashabiah	13. Shubael
	14. Mattithiah	15. Jeremoth
	16. Hananiah	17. Joshbekashah
	18. Hanani	19. Mallothi
	20. Eliathah	21. Hothir
	22. Giddalti	23. Maharioth
	24. Romamtiezer	

(7) Most interesting is the lack of congruence between the names in vss. 2-4a and vss. 9ff. The supposedly identical names in these two sections occur in slightly different form in their respective lists. The differences are not easily capable of simple resolution. However, there seems to be a rather definite tendency that the longer or more complete names are to be found in the list beginning with vs. 9, a list which has unanimously been accepted as a later addition.[65]

On the basis of an analysis of these names, I find it preferable to explain the linguistic differences by understanding the series of names in vss. 9ff. as having the more original forms. A further observation should be noted, that in vs. 4b the names are suddenly virtually identical to those in vss. 23ff. These are the very names which comprise the psalmette. This homogeneity of form is striking because if any names should have suffered in written transmission, it should have been these unusual formations.

The nature of the name differences already cited and the homogeneity of the hymnic names in both sections lead me to the conclusion that the redactor of the present chapter had two editions of Levitical singer lists, one already embedded in the basic Chronicles document—that is, vss. 2-4a—and one of linguistically earlier form in the hands of the redactor—vss. 9ff.—to which he added the Psalm fragment as names, thereby creating vs. 4b. To specify the nature of this redaction further, we should be aware that the division of the twenty-four singers depends on the redactor's division of the Levitical names, i.e. reading Romamtiezer as one name. Without his inclusion of the hymnic fragment as proper names, we would have no such divisional schema.

Here then at least two stages are visible in the present composition; however this is not the end of the business. On the basis of the earlier mentioned evidence for lack of unity, I would argue that we can discern the presence of three basic stages in the text. The oldest was most probably concerned just with Asaph. It included the mention of David and the separation of the sons of Asaph as well as the list of Asaph's sons in vs. 2, thereby explaining the absence of the numerical evaluation. A second development came with the insertion of the three-fold singer schema; this stage would have included most of vss. 1-4, 6-7. The third and final product would have embraced the emphasis on Heman, the appellation of Levitical singers as prophets, and the insertion of the hymnic fragment as names, and the division into twenty-four courses. I intentionally refrain from becoming too specific about each word as Rothstein has done because the evidence for different levels of redaction does not allow absolute division.

Where does 1 Chronicles 25 fit in Gese's traditio-historical analysis? The most obvious move would be to place it just before IIIB. While the name Jeduthun still appears, characteristic of IIIA, we find the dominant interest in Heman, characteristic of IIIB. However, such a synchronistic solution, Gese charges, ignores the comparison of 1 Chronicles 25 to the fourteen singer classes in 1 Chronicles 15:18, which he assigns to IIIB.[66] If 1 Chronicles 15:18ff. is later than 1 Chronicles 25, we would, he says, expect it to reflect the same or at least similar understanding of the service courses. However, this is hardly the case, since 1 Chronicles 15 speaks of only fourteen musicians distinguished on the basis of their instruments—eight harp players and six lyrists—whereas the courses in 1 Chronicles 25 are clearly based on the priestly pattern represented in 1 Chronicles 24. This argument based on the lack of correspondence between the two patterns of service is not convincing. The service courses of 1 Chronicles 25 are idiosyncratically based on an argument of a very specific sort (pro-Hemanite). It seems to me quite possible that the writer of 1 Chronicles 15 could have ignored the pattern created by the redactor of 1 Chronicles 25 since his material and purpose were not the same. The importance of the three names still seems primary. I would consequently classify 1 Chronicles 25 as part of IIIA, albeit late in this stage.

To summarize, this chapter presents us with a description of certain Levites, the singers, as prophets. The central focus is placed upon Heman, an emphasis which only appears in the redactional process. On the basis of redaction-critical study, we have discovered an editor at work, inserting a relevant hymn fragment into the Hemanite genealogy to further substantiate the claim to superior status for Levitical singers as prophets. The use of prophetic titles and material, the visions mentioned in the psalm fragment, and the claim for special attention for Heman appear to be interrelated.

C. Levitical Prophets and Holy War

From genealogies, we turn to a battle account, 2 Chronicles 20, in which Jehoshaphat, one of Judah's kings whom the Chronicler approves, is being challenged by a coalition approaching from the South. After a long speech appealing to Yahweh in time of extremity, the spirit of Yahweh descends upon Jahaziel, an Asaphite Levite who then prescribes the proper conduct for Israelite forces and forecasts the outcome of the battle. The war commences with songs of praise by the Korahites and ends in the total extermination of the coalition.

2 Chronicles 20:1-30

(1) And it happened that when the sons of Moab, and the sons of Ammon, as well as the Meunites[67] came to make war against Jehoshaphat, (2) messengers came and told Jehoshaphat, "A great force is coming from across the sea, from Edom.[68] They are already at Hazazontamar, that is Engedi." (3) Jehoshaphat was afraid and decided to seek the Lord. He proclaimed a fast in all Judah. (4) Judah gathered to seek Yahweh. All the cities of Judah came to seek the Lord. (5) Jehoshaphat stood in the congregation of Judah and Jerusalem in the house of the Lord, before the new court; (6) and he said, "O Lord God of our Fathers, are you not the God of the Heavens and the ruler of all the kingdoms of the nations? Are not power and strength in your hand so that no one can stand against you? (7) Have you not, our God, dispossessed the inhabitants of this land from before your people Israel and established the seed of your beloved Abraham forever? (8) And they dwelled in it and built for you a sanctuary for your name saying: (9) "If evil, the sword, flood,[69] pestilence, or hunger come upon us, we will stand before this house and before you, because your name is in this house; and we will cry out to you on account of our trouble; and you will hear and save us." (10) And now behold, the Ammonites, the Moabites, and those from Mt. Seir, whose countries you did not allow Israel to go into when they came out of Egypt since they turned aside from them and did not destroy them, (11) they pay us back in this way, by coming to drive us out from your possession which you gave to us as an inheritance. (12) O our God, will you not judge against them, because there is not sufficient strength in us against this great force which has come against us. Since we do not know what to do, our eyes are on you." (13) All Judah was standing before the Lord, even the little ones, wives, and sons. (14) Then the spirit of the Lord came upon Jahaziel, the son of Zechariah, the son of Beniah, the son of Jeiel, the son of Mattaniah, the Levite from the sons of Asaph, in the midst of the congregation, (15) and he said: "Pay attention all Judah and every inhabitant of Jerusalem and King Jehoshaphat. Thus says the Lord to you: Do not fear and do not be dismayed before this great force because the war is not yours but God's. (16) Tomorrow, go down against them, for they will come up at the valley of Ziz,[70] and you will find them at the end of the valley before the wilderness of Yeruel. (17) You do not have to fight in this battle. Just take up[71]your positions; stand and watch the salvation of the Lord on your behalf, O Judah and Jerusalem. Do not fear and do not be dismayed tomorrow. Go out against them and the Lord will be with you." (18) Then Jehoshaphat bowed his face, and all Judah and the inhabitants of Jerusalem fell down before the Lord to worship the Lord. (19) And the Levites of the Kohathites, more specifically the Korahites,[72]rose up in order to praise the Lord, the God of Israel, with a very loud voice; (20) and they got up early in the morning and went out to the wilderness of Tekoa. And while they were going out, Jehoshaphat stood and said, "Hear me, O Judah and citizens of Jerusalem, trust in the Lord your God and you will be vindicated. Trust in his prophets and you will be successful." (21) Having consulted with the people, he appointed singers in holy array [73]to praise the Lord as they went out before the troops saying, "Praise the Lord for his mercy is eternal." (22) And in the moment that they began to sing and to praise, the Lord set ambushes[74]against the sons of Ammon, Moab, and those of Mt. Seir, and they were struck down. (23) The sons of Ammon and Moab rose up to exterminate and destroy those from Mt. Seir. When they had finished off the inhabitants from Seir, each helped[75] to destroy the other. (24) When Judah came to a look-out point over the wilderness, they turned to look at the forces; and behold, there were fallen bodies on the ground; no survivors. (25) And when Jehoshaphat and his people came to plunder the spoils, they found many cattle,[76] goods, garments,[77] precious vessels; and they took for themselves more than could be carried. The plundering took three days since the spoil was so large.

(26) On the fourth day, they assembled together in the valley of Berechiah because there they blessed the Lord; therefore, they call the name of that place the valley of Berechiah up till today. (27) Then every man of Judah and Jerusalem returned, with Jehoshaphat in the lead,[78] to Jerusalem rejoicing because the Lord had given them pleasing results over their enemies; (28) and they came to Jerusalem with harps, zithers, and trumpets to the house of the Lord. (29) Consequently the fear of God was over all the kingdoms of the earth when they heard that the Lord had fought against the enemies of Israel. (30) The reign of Jehoshaphat was peaceful because his God gave him rest from all sides.

Before considering the interrelationship of Levites and prophecy, a major problem must be addressed: the historicity of the battle recorded in this chapter. Briefly stated, the author depicts an assembly of Moabites, Ammonites, and Meunites, who come up against Judah from the South. At first report, they are already in the vicinity of Engedi (Hazazontamar). After Jehoshaphat's cultic response, Judah goes out to find that the Moabites and Edomites have moved farther into the area near Tekoa, destroying the Meunites (now called the inhabitants of Mt. Seir)[79] and to witness the mutual self-destruction of Moab and Edom. The plunder of the battle is gathered in the valley of Berechiah, just south of Tekoa. This summary contains virtually all the topographic data given to us by the Chronicler—with the exception of vs. 16, Ziz and Yeruel. The problem is that this incident is presented to us only in Chronicles; there is no parallel account in the book of Kings.

Four kinds of solutions have been proposed to this apparent lack of consistency between Israel's two historical annals. The first or harmonizing solution is represented by Kautzsch, Wellhausen, and Benzinger. Their argument proceeds as follows: the mention of a fight against the Moabites requires 2 Kings 3 as a parallel.[80] Further the self-destruction of the enemy is a common element to both accounts. Consequently, the version in Chronicles should be viewed as an historical midrash on 2 Kings 3. Also, though the following point has never been made by the above commentators, in both 2 Kings 3 and 2 Chr 20, the activity of a prophet is bound up with the battle. Just as Elisha predicted the character of the victorious campaign against Moab, so Jahaziel gave instructions and predicted the outcome of the Judahite "campaign" against the southern coalition. This first solution has often been ignored by present commentators, though the nature of prophetic activity which is central to both accounts gives the argument more weight.

Second, Noth has argued at great length that the tale is based upon a local tradition. He is, as others, unimpressed by the scanty parallels between 2 Kings 3 and Chronicler's accounts; the specific place names induce him to argue that the account is not an invention out of whole cloth. Noth's thesis is quite simply that the place names, with the exception of those in vs. 16 which are no longer capable of precise identification, revolve around the Tekoa area. The mysterious Hazazontamar could refer to a terrace between Engedi and the coast of the Dead Sea or to an area ten kilometers north of Engedi on the way to the mountains.[81] Noth believes that the report is about an attack by early Nabataeans, Meun designating an area southeast of Petra in the

Edomitic Seir mountain chain, in either the latter half of the fourth century or the early part of the third.[82] The Chronicler's apparent familiarity with the material can only be explained by understanding this area as his homeland. Consequently, we should not think that there was a written version prior to the Chronicler's account. As for the relationship between the Chronicles and Kings passages, Noth says: "One can say at most, that the Chronicler has replaced the prophetic legend, 2 Kgs 3:4-27, by another only distantly comparable narrative, for which the basic stuff was supplied to him from a source unknown to us."[83]

Thirdly, Rudolph modifies Noth's position by contending: (1) that the term, Meunites, is occasioned by a desire to delimit more precisely the nature of the Edomites in the fight, i.e. that we need not seek so late a group as the Nabataeans; (2) that, against Noth, there was an Edomite coalition against Jehoshaphat as described in the Chronicler's narrative, while the Ammonites are there just to make a good third enemy; (3) that there was an earlier written version as shown by the Chronicler's explication of Hazazontamar by Engedi, i.e. that the source was more than a little-known local tradition; (4) that the dating c. 300 B.C. is unnecessary, even on Noth's grounds, because such early Nabataean elements could have been present as early as 400. The resort to these Nabataean Meunites is unnecessary. In other words, for Rudolph, ". . . the external circumstances of the tale in 2 Chronicles 20 rest on good tradition."[84] Myers apparently accepts Rudolph's modifications of Noth's argument.[85]

Most recently, Welten has argued that neither Rudolph's nor Noth's explanations suffice to explain the Chronicler's purpose in this and other chapters. In comparing 2 Chronicles 20 to 2 Chr 13:3-20 and 14:8-14, Welten has discovered a significant common theme, "battles of epic dimensions and extremely circumscribed geographic boundaries,"[86] battle reports which depict a very basic confrontation, not only military and political but also theological, for the post-exilic Israelite community. In 2 Chronicles 20, this conflict exists between the province of Judah and her Eastern neighbors. This programmatic style of history writing does not allow one to tie the battle description to a specific historical event.

It seems difficult to deny the force of Noth's contention that this battle story is set in a small section of land around Tekoa.[87] The questions of just who was involved and when the battle was fought are probably unanswerable today. The important question to be addressed to our text, however, does not deal with this historical question, whose answer remains uncertain. Nevertheless, with regard to the synoptic problem, one must, as does Noth, notice that the Chronicler has replaced the account of 2 Kings 3 with the modified local tradition in 2 Chronicles 20. The question we must answer is, Why has he done so? What did the Chronicler gain or achieve by the replacement of the older by the newer story? To answer this question, we now turn to consider this description of Jehoshaphat's war.

One of the most striking features of this text is the two speeches and the importance they have for the sequence of events resulting in the victory over the attacking nations.[88] The first of these is the so-called "prayer of Jehoshaphat." This section, vss. 3-15, seems remarkable because it fits into a pattern of Israelite cultic practice—the national lament accompanied by fasting and finally answered with a divine oracle (cf. especially 1 Kgs 8:21; Joel 1-2). Form-critics have long noted that a number of Psalms were probably used in such a way (Pss 44; 60; 74; 79; 83; 89).[89] The stereotypical features, following Eissfeldt's analysis of Ps 44, would be: the complaint—vss. 10-17, 20, 26, the plea for help—vss. 24-25, 27, the recitation of Yahweh's prior acts—vss. 5-9, protestations of innocence—vss. 18-19, 21-22, and the assertion that loyalty to Yahweh has brought on the disaster—vs. 23. We may easily identify many of these elements in the lament recited by Jehoshaphat: vss. 6-7—recitation of past favors, vss. 8-9—protestation of innocence and statement of trust, vss. 10-11—complaint, vs. 12—plea. However, two characteristics of this lament strike one as unusual. First, the use of the third person in vs. 8 and its implicit continuation in vs. 9, "Yahweh gave the land to the descendents of Abraham and they built the sanctuary saying . . . ," is unusual. It implies that the present generation had not and was not saying these sorts of things, that is, saying them on their own. The character of this quotation of the older generation is almost liturgical. I have in mind here an analogy in the way the Lord's Prayer is introduced into low liturgical traditions in the United States. The officiating clergy may say, ". . . and the prayer which our Lord taught us to pray saying, Our Father. . . ." Perhaps we have something of the same thing in this Chronicler's piece—the use of an earlier prayer, vs. 9. It is almost the theological precipitate of the national lament drama: "If trouble comes, we will go up to the temple which is the place where Yahweh's name is, and recite a prayer of lamentation, and receive an oracle of assurance." Vs. 9 is, in effect, a summary of the whole proceedings included within one of the elements of the cultic lament act.

Second, the plethora of questions in the introductory section of the lament deviates from the stereotypic pattern. When the deeds of old are recited, these are thought to be the data of faith, Ps 74:13, "You divided the sea with your strength and broke the heads of the dragons of the waters." Yet, in Jehoshaphat's prayer these acts are more general than in other laments: vs. 6, "In your hand are power and might, so that none is able to withstand you." Further, in this text, these assertions are phrased as questions, a literary device almost never found in laments. Questions, to be sure, are part of the national lament pattern, but they occur as a part of the plea: Who will help? How long, O Lord? (cf. Pss 60:9-10; 74:1-2, 10; 79:5; 80:4; 89:46, 48; as well as 2 Chr 20:12). One could dismiss the questions as rhetorical questions. But such a dismissal ignores the character of rhetorical questions. The device is intended to create a deeper impression on the hearer than would have been obtained by making a direct statement.[90] To see this effect at work in our text, we must follow what the writer has done by passing over rather lightly the three general questions asserting the power of Yahweh and focus on the final one, that Yahweh drove the inhabitants of the land away. It is upon this element, contrasted to the earlier and more general claims that the element of recitation in the lament rests. And this very element serves as a foil or counterpoise to the subject of the complaint: Yahweh's sin of omission. He did rid Israel of those in the land, but not those outside of the land. In this method of contrasts, the author of this lament has used the recitation of Yahweh's prior deeds to heighten Israel's complaint, both against the enemy and against Yahweh.

Inserted between the two speeches is the introduction to Jahaziel. 2 Chr 20:14 presents us with two facts which defend one basic contention: Jehaziel is a Levitical prophet. First, the "spirit of Yahweh" descends upon Jahaziel. This is, as Mowinckel has argued, a paradigmatic way of denoting prophetic authority in the pre- and post-classical descriptions of prophetic activity.[91] Jahaziel is a prophet because he has received Yahweh's spirit. Then vs. 14 proceeds to Jahaziel's genealogy, a genealogy in which, though explicit derivation of Mattaniah from Asaph himself is avoided, Jahaziel's pedigree is traced back to the time of David, viz. through the time of Jehoshaphat, Asa, Abijah, Rehoboam to the united monarchy.[92]

Moving to the second speech, vss. 15-17, we find another part of the national lament ritual, the oracle of mercy,[93] the answer to the complaint. Scholars have suggested that the more positive attitude which often ends such sections represents an answer by some cult official. This explains the sudden change of tone in national laments. Begrich's study of the priestly oracle of salvation provided the analogies by which we now understand this cultic response. In the simplest form the saying has three parts: (1) the phrase "Fear not" (Lam 3:57); (2) the designation of the addressed party (Isa 41:10); (3) the assurance that Yahweh was heard (Isa 41:14).[94] This basic form underwent many permutations as it was revised by Israelite prophets. Pertinent to our Chronicles text is the fact that vs. 15 mirrors the early form of the priestly salvation oracle; all three of the basic elements are present. The parties are most explicitly designated, the phrase "Fear not" is present (also in the reprise, vs. 17), and the assurance is given in a promise of battle support. This oracle is the very sort of answer we should expect from the national cultic lament pattern. The oracle is, of course, a literary artifice constructed to fit specifically into this narrative context.[95] But it is noteworthy that the Chronicler has used an ancient form to present Jahaziel's response.

The only problem in letting our analysis end with this last element of the public lament is that the narrative continues. Simply to label 2 Chr 20:3-17 a public lament, as Eissfeldt has done, ignores its place in the story of Jehoshaphat's war. A more perceptive reading of Jahaziel's speech allows us to see that the Chronicler was interested in presenting more than just a lament. This speech represents a turning, not a break; for it, as well as several earlier parts of the chapter, may be viewed within the context of one of Israel's oldest institutions, the holy war. The "Fear not" formula signals this genre (cf. Exod 14:13; Josh 8:1; 10:8; 1 Sam 23:16), and thereby opens up the passage for further analysis of these apparently melded forms: national lament and holy war.[96]

At this point, we may retreat for a moment and review the earlier parts of the chapter. The people, though not the ^{c}m yhwh of old, have assembled in Jerusalem. Instead of a short query as to the success of the operation, e.g. 1 Sam 14:37, we find a long lament of Jehoshaphat which functions as the shorter question since it draws out the divine answer about the future of the war. Jahaziel's speech then functions in two ways: as the salvation oracle in the lament pattern and as the divine decision about Yahweh's action in the holy war.

Von Rad argues, surely correctly, that the phrases "the battle is not yours but Yahweh's," (vs. 15) and "take your positions, stand still, and see the victory of the Lord on your behalf," (vs. 17) echo respectively 1 Sam 17:47 where in challenging Goliath David says, "the battle is Yahweh's" and Exod 14:13 where Moses, at the edge of the Red Sea says to the Israelites, "Fear not, stand firm, and see the salvation of the Lord."[97] This speech is replete with features of the holy war ideology: the perfect certainty of victory, it is Yahweh's war, Yahweh will fight for them, Israel shall not fear but believe.[98] These elements all indicate the attempt by the Chronicler to relate this narrative to one of Israel's oldest traditions.

As the story continues, the pattern of the holy war undergoes a major revision with the result that the purpose of the writer becomes much clearer. We would normally expect the battle scene with confusion wrought upon the enemy. This comes to be sure, but in vs. 23. In between vs. 23 and the preparation, we have a further preparatory interlude, the interjection of an element foreign to the older accounts. The author has placed a new party of functionaries before us, the Korahites and Kohathites, and it is with this group that the narrative is bound up until the battle is won.

Following the introduction of this group into the scene, Jehoshaphat delivers an admonition. The first element, "Believe in the Lord your God and you will be established," is a normal and expected part of the holy war procedure, though such admonitions to faith are usually connected with the phrase "Fear not."[99] One is strongly tempted to see this phrase as a direct borrowing from Isa 7:9b.[100] Isaiah had been directed to speak to Ahaz as he faced a Syro-Ephraimitic coalition. At the end of an oracle intended to hearten Ahaz, Isaiah says, ". . . if you will not believe, surely you shall not be established." In this case, the negative phrasing seems to prefigure the negative response of Ahaz. In 2 Chr 20, the threatening quality is mitigated. The phrase is cast in positive terms. Furthermore, instead of being a counsel from prophet to king, the phrase is now used as an admonition from king to people.

Then in nicely parallel fashion, we find Jehoshaphat adjuring the gathered assembly to "believe in his prophets and you will succeed." It is difficult to view this as anything more than a most innovative and unusual claim. There are at least three facets to this assertion—all three of which can, I think, be accepted as integral to the Chronicler's purpose. Initially, he is calling attention to the fact that the phrase's basic claim—"believe in the Lord your God and you will be established"—is a claim not of his own making. It is a claim made within Israel's past, a claim now known in a collection of Isaiah's words, albeit here in a slightly altered form. Further, a prophetic figure, Jahaziel, has just spoken to Israel as a part of the holy war pattern, and his message demands attentive obedience. Finally, the Korahites have the same authority as the Asaphite singers (see below) and carry, for the Chronicler, a prophetic force. To believe in their activity in the ensuing battle is also required.

Following the narrative, Jehoshaphat designates individuals to perform the singing, surely the singers mentioned in vs. 19, and gives them the text for their song or chant: "Give thanks to the Lord, for his steadfast love endures forever." And then the battle begins, or more accurately, and then the song of praise commences, for at the very moment these Levitical singers strike up the song, Yahweh wreaks havoc upon the enemy. This I take to be the crucial point of the story—that the Korahite singers are those responsible for bringing Israel to the victory.[101] This choral activity constituted prophecy by the Levitical singers; such was post-exilic prophecy in the Chronicler's eyes.

It is instructive to compare again the more traditional elements of the holy-war procedure with the action described in 2 Chronicles 20. Normally, the battle is begun with a war cry.[102] In our narrative, this cry has been altered into a more cultic, or with von Rad, spiritual form. Instead of the $t^e r\hat{u}^c \bar{a}h$ (e.g. Judg 7:20), we now have a Psalmic chant. And instead of the entire company uttering the battle cry, a group of cultic officials was designated for the task.

Von Rad provides a concise summary:

> The cultic . . . has now become again, through the emphasis on the varied divine service celebrations, the most important characteristic of the whole. . . . Above all, the supporting function, which is now incumbent on the cultic personnel, is noteworthy. The characteristic of the older holy war was that it was carried out with a minimum of extra officials. In opposition, here a large apparatus of cultic officials functions; and it creates the impression that the divine help dovetails exactly with the entrance of the cultic activity.[103]

We end our examination of the narrative from the holy war perspective by observing that nothing is said about the *ḥerem*. Instead, a service of praise was held on the battlefield, and then repeated in Jerusalem,—a service of harps, lyres, and trumpets (yet another implicit mention of the Levitical prophets' activity, cf. 1 Chr 15:16ff.).

One further problem remains after we have seen the way in which the Chronicler has revised the holy war model to emphasize the place of the Levitical singers as prophets, and that is an attempt to fit this story into the tradition-history schema of Gese. The complicating feature is that the typical names of Levitical singers present, when the normal traditions allow of two groups, are Asaph and Jeduthun. In 2 Chronicles 20 we have two groups, but they are described as Asaphite and Korahite. Since there are only two groups accounted as Levites, the story must represent a stage prior to IIIA. And since the two groups are presupposed, the classification could not predate stage II. The necessary question is asked by Gese: are the Korahite singers in 2 Chr 20:19 now identical with the Jeduthun group? He answers: since the Jeduthun group continues on from stage II, only to appear in IIIB with another name, we must assume that in 2 Chronicles 20 the Jeduthun group is implied (along with the Korahites). That one may assign a Korahite to the Jeduthun group, we are able to ascertain in the case of Obed-Edom, who is listed as a Korahite in 1 Chr 26:4, 8, 15 and as a member of the Jeduthun group in 1 Chr 15:18 (21). For some reason, the more prevalent name, Jeduthun, was used as a pseudonym for the increasingly powerful Korahite group.

Gese contends that to understand fully the character of this emphasis on the Korahites we must recall the well-known rebellion of Korah in Numbers 16.[104] This chapter must surely reflect some of the strife in late exilic or post-exilic cultic status. According to this interpretive perspective, the Korahites sought to achieve priestly status and were refused. And since the priestly office was thus closed to them, the only possibility for cultic status would have been in the Levitical offices, specifically that of Levitical singers. Gese goes on to suggest that we may explain the existence of the Hemanite group within this context. 1 Chr 6:18ff. and Ps 88 make it clear that the Hemanites derive from Korah. And in stage IIIB, we see that the Hemanites grow strong as the Asaphite group is pushed into the background. Gese thus argues that 2 Chr 20:19 reflects a period just prior to IIIA, when this Korah group was gaining strength but was not yet the cohesive group of Heman in IIIB. In this period before IIIA, the non-Asaphites were called . . . *min-benê haqqehātîm* since there may have been non-Korahites in the Jeduthun group. So Gese contends, "The characterization of the non-Asaphite singers as descending from Korah could have been taken over by the Chronicler as a genealogical designation; this is surely true for Heman and at least partially the case for Jeduthun."[105]

We are now left with the task of summarizing the varied emphases and directions noted in this chapter of 2 Chronicles. First, it is an especially important chapter. Plöger has demonstrated that prayers and speeches denote significant moments in the deuteronomistic and Chronistic historical works.[106] 2 Chronicles 20 is replete with a long prayer and a salvation oracle. The Chronicler has underlined the chapter in red by his use of this device. Secondly, we have seen two formal patterns—the national lament and the holy war—appropriated by the writer to depict an event. Thirdly, the chapter is less an historical description, in its present state, than it is an occasion for describing the character of the Levitical singers in the Chronicler's day. The success of the war is directly linked to the functioning of the Asaphite and Korahite Levites, both of whom are described as prophets. The chapter is not an historical midrash in the normally accepted use of that term. The Chronicler evidently had some tradition of a local battle in the region of Tekoa which he was able to use in place of the 2 Kings 3 report of Elisha's activity in the context of a war against Moab. Concern over the historicity of the battle is less fruitful than the concern over the redaction-critical issue. The Chronicler has not only substituted one war story for another, but he has also substituted one prophetic legend for another tale depicting not the actions of a popular prophetic figure but describing the character of prophecy in his own day. The text is a retrojection: how the Asaphites and Korahites would have functioned in Israel's past. As such, 2 Chr 20 is a crucial instance in which the Chronicler presents us with a glimpse of how post-exilic prophecy was conceived by the hierocratic elements. By writing history in this way, the Chronicler helped substantiate the Levitical singers' claim to cultic authority as prophets in post-exilic society.

D. Hezekiah's Temple Cleansing and the Levites

The final major text to which we turn our attention, 2 Chronicles 29, is a narrative about royal initiative and consequent response from cultic officials. Hezekiah, another king favored by the Chronicler, sponsored a passover well-known to those concerned with the historical development of that cultic practice. However, the preparatory purification of the temple and officials is usually overlooked in the study of this passover celebration; in this episode a narrator gives attention to the Levites, and calls one of the Levitical singers "prophet."

2 Chronicles 29

(1) Hezekiah began to rule when he was twenty-five years old, and he reigned twenty-nine years in Jerusalem. The name of his mother was Abijah, the daughter of Zechariah. (2) He acted uprightly according to all which his father David had done. (3) In the first month of the first year of his reign,[107] he opened the doors of the house of the Lord and repaired them. (4) And he brought the priests and the Levites and gathered them to the eastern plaza,[108] (5) and he said to them, "Hear me, O Levites; sanctify yourselves now and sanctify the house of the Lord, the God of your fathers; and bring out the impurity from the holy place, (6) because our fathers were unfaithful and acted wickedly in the eyes of the Lord our God and abandoned him and turned their faces from the dwelling of the Lord and turned their backs. (7) They even shut the doors of the porch and extinguished the lamps and did not burn incense or offer burnt offerings in the holy place of the God of Israel. (8) Consequently, the anger of the Lord is upon Judah and Jerusalem; and it has made them a terror, a desolation, and a derision, as you can see with your own eyes. (9) Behold, our fathers fell by the sword and our sons, daughters, and wives were in captivity because of this.[109] (10) Now it is in my heart to make a covenant with the Lord God of Israel so that his violent wrath may turn away from us. (11) Now, my sons, do not be negligent because the Lord has chosen you to stand before him, to serve and to be servants and incense burners for him." (12) Then the Levites arose—Mahath the son of Amasi, and Joel the son of Azariah, of the sons of the Kohathites; and of the sons of Merari, Kish the son of Abdi, and Azariah the son of Jehallelel; and of the Gershonites, Joah the son of Zimmah, and Eden the son of Joah; (13) and of the sons of Elizaphan, Shimri and Jeuel; and of the sons of

Asaph, Zechariah and Mattaniah; (14) and of the sons of Heman, Jehuel and Shimei; and of the sons of Jeduthun, Shemaiah and Uzziel—(15) and they gathered their brothers, sanctified themselves, and went to clean the house of the Lord according to the command of the king by the words of the Lord.[110] (16) And the priests entered the inside of the house of the Lord, to clean it; and they brought out all the unclean things which they found in the temple of the Lord to the court of the house of the Lord; and the Levites received it to take it outside to the Kidron valley. (17) They began to sanctify on the first day of the month. By the eighth day of the month, they had come to the porch of the Lord. Then they sanctified the house of the Lord eight more days, and on the sixteenth day[111] of the first month they had completed the work. (18) They went in before Hezekiah the king and said, "We have cleaned all of the house of the Lord: the altar for the burnt offering, all its vessels, and the table for the rows of bread and all its vessels; (19) and all the vessels which Ahaz the king rejected during his apostate reign, we have prepared and consecrated; and they are now before the altar of the Lord." (20) Hezekiah the king rose early and gathered the princes of the town and went up to the house of the Lord. (21) They brought seven bulls, seven rams, seven lambs, and seven he-goats as a sin offering for the monarchy, for the sanctuary, and for Judah. He commanded the sons of Aaron, the priests, to offer them up on the altar of the Lord. (22) And they killed the bulls and the priests received the blood and sprinkled it upon the altar. They slaughtered the rams and sprinkled the blood upon the altar; and they killed the sheep and scattered the blood upon the altar; (23) and they brought the goats for the sin offering before the king; and the congregation set their hands upon them. (24) The priests killed them and made a sin offering with the blood on the altar to atone for all Israel because the king had commissioned a burnt offering and a sin offering for all Israel. (25) He set the Levites in the house of the Lord with cymbals, harps, and zithers according to the command of David, Gad the seer of the king, and Nathan the prophet, because by the hand of Yahweh the command was by the hand of his prophets.[112] (26) And the Levites stood with the instruments of David, and the priests had the trumpets; (27) then Hezekiah ordered the burnt offerings to be offered on the altar. With the beginning of the offering, the song of the Lord and the trumpeting also began, accompanied by[113] the instruments of David, king of Israel. (28) The entire congregation worshipped. And the singers continued to sing and the trumpeters kept on trumpeting until the burnt offering was finished. (29) And when the burnt offering was completed, the king and those with him bowed down and prostrated themselves. (30) Then Hezekiah the king and the princes ordered the Levites to praise the Lord with the words of David and Asaph the seer, and they sang praises with great joy and bowed down and prostrated themselves. (31) Hezekiah said, "Now that you have devoted yourselves[114] to the Lord, come near and bring sacrifices and thank offerings to the house of the Lord." And the congregation brought sacrifices and thank offerings, and all who had a willing spirit brought burnt offerings. (32) The number of burnt offerings which the congregation brought was: seventy bulls, one hundred rams, two hundred lambs; all these were as burnt offerings for Yahweh. (33) The dedicated offerings amounted to six hundred bulls and three thousand sheep. (34) However, there were too few priests. Since they were unable to flay the burnt-offerings, their comrades, the Levites, aided them until the work was finished and until the priests consecrated themselves. For the Levites were more dedicated in consecrating themselves than the priests. (35) As well as the great abundance of burnt offerings there were the pieces of fat from the peace offering and the libations for the burnt-offering; thus was the service of the Lord established. (36) Hezekiah and all the people rejoiced over what the Lord had done for the people, because it was accomplished so quickly.

Hezekiah's temple cleansing seems, on the face of it, an innocuous event, an incident in which we would not expect the Chronicler to take any great interest. However, this one chapter, closely connected to the famous narration of Hezekiah's passover, is highly complex, perhaps more so than any other text this study investigates. That it is connected to the passover plot of Hezekiah, a story which the Chronicler tells in a version very different from that of the Deuteronomist, gives us an inkling of this chapter's importance.

Briefly summarized, it portrays Hezekiah as initiating the cleansing of the temple by calling certain cultic officials and telling them to sanctify the temple. Then, after a short genealogy of the Levites, it tells how the temple was rededicated. From vss. 20ff., a variety of sacrifices prepared by uncertain parties is described. It is in this section that the greatest difficulty lies. Here occurs the reference to Levitical prophets (vs. 25).

We will begin our analysis by calling attention to the audience-designations; in vs. 4 the audience is referred to as "priests and Levites" but in vs. 5, as "Levites." Many critics have at this point begun the search for other signs to prove that there are two traditions in the text, traditions which depict the role of the Levites as distinct from the more composite "priests and Levites," (e.g. Welch, *The Work of the Chronicler*, pp. 103ff.). A brief overview shows, in fact, that there is evidence of two such traditions. In vs. 12 only the Levites are addressed when a Levitic genealogy is introduced. There is a rather clear-cut division between priestly responsibility in vss. 20-24 and Levitical activity in vss. 12, 25-30. Finally, vs. 34 indicates some tension between Levites and priests: the priests were unable to prepare all of the burnt offerings and required help from the Levites. The writer uses this state of affairs to comment that the Levites had been more rigorous in preparation than had the priests. The final product, 2 Chronicles 29, represents more than just a simple description of Hezekiah's temple rededication; we have probable cause to suspect special interests represented in this chapter.

The first issue in a detailed examination of this chapter is the speech of Hezekiah. Keeping in mind Plöger's thesis that speeches indicate what is important in the Chronicler's work, how do we evaluate the importance of Hezekiah's speech? The Chronicler is arguing that an event, the rededication, is important and that Hezekiah is to be accorded special approbation. But these rather obvious inferences ignore the content of the speech. As we have noted, the juxtaposition of the first line of that speech with the prior description of the audience, priests and Levites, is quite revealing. On the basis of "Hear me, O Levites," (vs. 5) the Levites become the sole addressees. The admonition to self-sanctification and to the removal of the filth from the temple is closely tied with what the Levites are depicted as having done in vss. 15-16. It is striking that this charge to the Levites dovetails so neatly with the narrative's description of what they did: the carrying of the *ṭumʾāh/niddāh*. Furthermore, this charge does not stipulate the role of the priests as depicted in vs. 16a—carrying the *ṭumʾāh* from the holy of holies to the outer court. After the introductory charge, the speech chronicles the cultic sins of the fathers (vss. 6-8) and then recounts the consequences that Israel had experienced (vss. 8-9). Vs. 10 presents a statement of Hezekiah's intention to form a new covenant to break the pattern of retribution.[115] And then vs. 11 returns to the addressee—the Levites—and gives them a four-fold task: not to be negligent, to minister, to be ministers,[116] and to burn incense, correcting the omission of incense offering in the past (vs. 7).

"Incense" is the context in which I wish to discuss this section of the Chronicler's narrative. The definitive work on incense in the Ancient Near East and in the Hebrew Bible has yet to be written. The force of the charge against the fathers for not having burned incense is somewhat unclear because we do not fully understand the prescribed incense rites. According to Haran, three cultic rites used incense: (1) the use of spice as a supplement to a meal offering;[117] (2) the censer-incense rite, and performed in long-handled censers within the general temple precinct apparently limited to the Aaronite priesthood (P in Num 16:40), though Haran is unclear here; and (3) the altar incense rite, *qᵉṭōret hassammîm*, limited to the incense or gold altar and performed by the High Priest.[118]

Unfortunately, Haran did not include Chronicles in his study; consequently, the descriptions of incense practices in Chronicles do not easily conform to the categories. In 2 Chr 26:16-20, a text describing the *raison d'être* for Uzziah's leprosy, the incense ritual does not reflect Haran's divisions. Uzziah plans to burn incense on the incense altar (vs. 16), but he also has a censer in his hand (vs. 19). The text seems to represent a conflation of Haran's types two and three: the censer and the main altar rites. As for 2 Chronicles 29, since the appellative *sammîm* is absent, a term requisite for the altar-incense rite, we should understand this rite to be the censer practice. And if the text does describe the censer ritual, it is a ritual which should be limited to the Aaronite priesthood. But here again, the Chronicler does not reflect Haran's categories or the Priestly formulations (Num 16:40) because 2 Chr 29:11 clearly suggests that the Levites are to be given the right to burn the censer incense. Chronicles contravenes the Priestly regulations.

At least one tradition insisted that the censer sacrifice was to be limited to the sons of Aaron (Num 16:40). Haran has studied the Nadab and Abihu (Aaron's eldest sons) account in Lev. 10:1-3 and has argued correctly that the point of this story is that improper fire was used to ignite the censers; Nadab's fire did not come from cultically acceptable flames. He contends that the same holds true for the Dathan and Abiram episode in the Korah rebellion (Numbers 16); the issue is not who performs the censer rite but how it is done. With this interpretation of Numbers 16 I can not agree, especially since Haran ignores the differing narrative strands of this difficult chapter. The JE story of Dathan and Abiram has nothing to do with either censers or incense. It is only in the P traditions that these issues become important. In the original P version, Korah is challenged by Moses to a trial by fire and incense (vs. 6—doublet in P_2, vs. 17). The censers were lit (vs. 8, P_1) and fire consumed the Korah group (vs. 35, P_1). It was left to the P_2 redactor for editorial comment, which he gave in vs. 40: no one but the Aaronite priests may burn incense, not the *qᵉṭōret hassammîm*, but the ordinary censer incense offering. Korah suffers for two reasons: he is smitten because he tried to achieve priestly status in P_1 and, according to P_2, because he offered incense. The issue is thus a bit more complicated than Haran would have us believe. In neither the JE nor the P versions does the issue appear to be the result of the wrong fire being used, as Haran contends. Instead, a dominant Priestly concern is the preservation of the censer ritual for the Aaronites.[119] The Chronicler, in 2 Chronicles 29, is arguing against such a position by contending that the Levites should have the right to burn the censer incense.

The relationship between the Korah rebellion and our text is deeper than just the issue of incense. This pivotal episode in Numbers deals with the very group which is important in the portrayal of the Levitical singers in Chronicles: the Korahites. We should not ignore the small P_2 addition in Num 16:1, "the son of Kohath, son of Levi," for this is the very group who responded to the speech of Hezekiah—in vs. 22 explicitly and, as argued earlier, perhaps in vs. 14 implicitly—as a part of the Heman/Jeduthun construct. If we may assume that the final redaction of Numbers 16 is not distant chronologically from the Chronicler's text, we may have reflected in Num 16 a viewpoint rather different from that supposed in Chronicles, a difference based upon varying evaluations of the Levitical role in cultic affairs, especially of the role played by the Levitical groups called singers and prophets in the Chronicler's narrative. The Priestly redactor does not approve full Levitical involvement, whereas the Chronicler is defending increased rights for the Levites.

Moving back to 2 Chronicles 29, we note that the genealogy presented to us in vss. 12-14 is odd. We are given the three classic Levitic tribes: first, Kohath, then Elizaphan, no stranger to such lists (e.g. 1 Chr 15:8); and finally a tripartite division of the Levitical singers, this time as Asaph, Heman, and Jeduthun (the names and ordering of Gese's phase IIIA). In comparison with the 1 Chronicles 15 list, the three singer divisions replace Hebron and Uzziel in vss. 9-10. As Möhlenbrink has noted, Kohath is accorded the signal position in this genealogy as he is in 1 Chronicles 6 and 15:5.[120] Möhlenbrink infers that the division represents a reworking of the classic patterns to fit the reality of the Chronicler's times, i.e. that the Kohathite line had achieved greater status than they had earlier. The genealogy is probably to be viewed as an insertion into the narrative and is intended to show the importance of these Kohathites and to reflect the growing significance of the singers, though not the apogee of the influence. This stage is visible in 1 Chronicles 6 where the Heman group (the most important singer group in IIIB) has been assimilated into the Kohathite genealogy, a genealogy which includes Korah.

The narrative of chapter 29 says that "they" began the work. Whether "they" originally meant both priests and Levites or only Levites is now impossible to determine. Within the final redaction, both are implied. In the very next verse the priests are described as entering the temple.

Some have taken the mention of both priests and Levites in vs. 16 to be a degrading of the Levites. Though for the Chronicler Kidron is a place for the destruction of improper cultic objects (cf. 2 Chr 15:16 where Asa has an Asherah demolished at Kidron, and 2 Chr 30:14 which describes a populist iconoclasm under Hezekiah, the destruction of incense altars at Kidron), the inference that because the Levites carried out the dirty work of the priests and went to an unclean place where they themselves became unclean is not legitimate. In neither 2 Chr 15:16 nor 2 Chr 30:14 do the parties become contaminated by their activity at Kidron. Further, since the Levites are presented as eager helpers to the priests in 2 Chr 29:34, this readiness to do the dirty work of the priests was probably intended to redound to the glory of the Levites.[121]

The reinstitution of the sacrificial system poses the most difficult questions in the chapter. It appears that three separate rites are described: sin and burnt offering (vss. 20-24), burnt offering (vss. 25-30), a random assortment of sacrifices (vss. 31-36). Let it be said that some commentators see this string of descriptions as a harmonious whole.[122] However, many others have been struck by the hodgepodge of the sacrificial lists. Of the three aforementioned divisions, the first (sin offering) has received the most attention because of its anomalous statements about the involved parties. Briefly stated, Hezekiah and the officials of the city bring a number of animals up to the temple for a sacrifice. Hezekiah is quoted as ordering "the priests, the sons of Aaron" to offer them on the altar of the Lord. From then on, vss. 22f., no other group is mentioned, thereby implying that the priests were responsible for both the killing and the manipulation of the blood. But for several reasons, the matter is not quite that simple. First, the priests are said to receive the blood. If the priests slew the animals, then it makes little sense to talk about priests receiving the blood, especially since the subject of vs. 22a — "they killed" — is not defined and is followed by "the priests received." This anomaly has resulted in several theories. Hänel thought that in an earlier version of this text, the king and people slaughtered the animals and then gave over the animals for sacrifice, whereas the redactor wanted to show that the laity were responsible for the killing.[123] This argument, that the phrase "the priests the sons of Aaron" is an addition, makes a good deal of sense. It seems odd to find the priests designated in the latter part of vs. 21, referred to generally in vs. 22a, and then specified again as "the priests" in the next clause. We should thus understand "the sons of Aaron" in vs. 21 to be an insertion and most probably "the priests" as well. The implication of this earlier version is that the slaughter was accomplished by the king and the officials while the priests were responsible for the blood rite.

To defend this early lay-slaughter theory, we need to turn to the Priestly laws concerning the ʿōlāh in Leviticus 1. In vs. 4, it is quite clear that after the laying on of the hands, the person giving the animal for the burnt offering kills the animal. Then Aaron's sons, the priests, Lev 1:4, manipulate the blood.[124] If the sacrifices in vss. 20-24 had been performed according to the prescriptions in Leviticus, the king and his officials would have slaughtered the goat and presented the blood to the priests. 2 Chr 29:24 states that this was not the case, that the priests both killed the animals and manipulated the blood on the altar.

Hence, in the final product, 2 Chr 29:20-24, we may observe an important step in the evolution of sacrificial practice. In opposition to the regulations of Leviticus, there was a tendency to make the Aaronite priesthood responsible for both the slaying of the burnt offering and the sin offering as well as to preserve their traditional blood manipulation ritual. Vs. 24 depicts a move away from lay slaughter to slaughter by priests.

We turn next to a section where the interest centers primarily on the burnt offering even though the sin offering is present, vss. 25-30. Here the dominant cultic functionaries are now the Levites. Unlike vss. 20-24, the description in vss. 25-30 gives the impression of being a relatively cohesive unit. The writer has gone to some trouble to make clear that the Levitical praise is of critical importance to this cultic act.

2 Chr 29:25-30 raises two central questions: First, is the burnt offering the same as the one described in vss. 20-24 or are we presented with two separate events? This is exceptionally difficult to answer. The best responses, positive and negative, are those of Welch and Rudolph respectively. Welch argues that vss. 20-24 and vss. 25-30 represent different ceremonies—burnt offering with sin offering and burnt offering, with concomitantly different emphases on the cultic officials in each of the stories.[125] Rudolph has stated that even with these difficulties, the Chronicler's basic purpose was to show the simultaneity of the Levitical action: the singing with the burnt offering.[126]

I propose a harmonistic solution, accepting both answers. I think it is clear that we have two originally separate episodes. The presence of the sin offering in vss. 20-24 is not integrated with vss. 25-30 which depict the performance of the prophetic song. However, the final product, vss. 2-30, functions as a continuous whole for a reason that even Rudolph overlooked. If we turn back to the description of the burnt offering in Lev 1:4-9, we discover that the blood rite is not the final part of the burnt-offering sacrifice. The burning itself completes the cultic action; into this sequence of blood rite and altar burning the Chronicles redactor has fitted the two components: sin offering and burnt offering.

The second basic question is this: how are we to understand the role of the prophetic figures and appellations in this section? In answer, it must be noted that something more is at stake than just an appeal to prophetic titles. The name of David appears four times in these verses. Thus, it is quite apparent that the author is trying to achieve authority for his prophetic descriptions. The Davidic appeal is used to sanction the Levitical instruments (vss. 25-27, the same instruments as those in the important passage, 1 Chronicles 25) and the words of praise (vs. 30). David provides the ultimate sanction which then proceeds through the penultimate, prophetic figures to the Chronicler's generation. Surely this conception of authority is at work in the difficult phrase at the end of vs. 25, explaining how the commandments of David and

Yahweh work together in the messages of Gad and Nathan. Likewise, Asaph and David share the authority for the words of praise, i.e., probably Asaphite psalms.

What is truly remarkable about this passage is the identification of the roles of Asaph and Gad (vss. 25, 30). The presence of Nathan and Gad with the differing titles of "prophet" and "seer" is interesting (though this difference between "prophet" and "seer," especially in late material, can be overemphasized).[127] This application of "seer" to Asaph is as explicit a statement of intention by the Chronicler as is possible. Asaph, the first, and in the early stages, the most important of the Levitical singers, is called "seer," a move which creates a direct link between prophetic action and the activity of the Levites in this section. Hence, vss. 25-30 are to be understood as descriptions of prophetic activity. The goal of the author seems to have been an equation of the roles of the Levitic progenitors with the functions of the early court prophets; his motive was to give the Levitical singers Davidic authority for their "prophetic" activity, the songs of praise in the cult.

Finally, we turn to the last section of this chapter, vss. 31-36. Three items are noteworthy. First, the collection of sacrificial offerings is not clear. Whether or not the *waw* introducing *tôdôt* is epexegetical is moot. Lev 7:12 states that a peace offering may be given as either a *tôdāh*, a *nēder* or a *nᵉdābāh*, that is, as a thanksgiving, a votive, or a freewill offering. Rudolph's attempt to subsume *qodāšim*, *šᵉlāmîm*, and *tôdāh* under the rubric *ᶜōlāh* seems forced.[128] We know little more about the *qodāšim* than that they were offerings over which the Levites could have specific charge (2 Chr 31:12; 35:13), even in their more generic and perhaps non-sacrificial sense (1 Chr 26:20, 26; 28:12). Whichever way we divide up or classify these offerings, the author had one intention: to show that the temple sacrificial system had been reinstituted in a fully successful fashion. Whether, as Rudolph asserts, the covenant is to be seen as implicitly renewed is difficult to say.[129] We do not have the divine affirmation in the form of a consuming fire, as it appeared in 2 Chronicles 5. The emphasis is less on covenant than on the role of the Levites in the reestablishment of the sacrifices.

A second problem reflects the issue of lay versus priestly participation. Hezekiah states that a group, though undefined, has consecrated itself. In vs. 31b, we find the assembly themselves bringing the sacrifices called for in vs. 31a. And the offerings of *haqqāhāl* are the two types of *zebah* offering: the thanksgiving and the freewill offering (Lev 7:11ff.). There is a shift of sacrificial terminology in vs. 32. The congregation is not depicted as bringing the burnt offering, and then the more general *qodāšîm* in vs. 33. Switching back to the burnt offering in vs. 33, the Chronicler speaks of the difficulty the priests were having in flaying the animals (cf. 2 Chr 30:3, 15-17). When we look back to the laws in Leviticus, this change is strange since Lev 1:6 implies that the offerer of the sacrifice is to flay the animal himself. Clearly, the verse disrupts the theme of the lay participation in the sacrifices begun earlier in this section.

Third, the Chronicler focuses on the continuing theme of the prominence of certain Levites. He has adeptly used two themes, the plethora of sacrifices in the reinstituted cult and the necessity for cultic aides to create a context for his statement about the Levites in vs. 34. As pointed out, vs. 34 seems to be out of order; it would appear more appropriate after vs. 32. The verse itself contradicts stipulated sacrificial practice (cf. Lev 1:6 and above). The author must have synthesized statements like 2 Chr 30:3 and 2 Chr 35:11 from two separate Passover celebrations to create the charge against the priests stated here. That 2 Chr 29:34 is anti-priestly seems hard to deny.[130]

What then may be said about this chapter, especially about vss. 20ff.? Most importantly, the chapter is another instance of the use of prophetic titles and authority to describe the Levitical singers' work in the post-exilic cult. The author of this chapter was intent on describing Hezekiah's temple rededication in a way most conducive to giving Levites, and more particularly the Levitical singers, power. To make this point, the author has conflated several sacrificial practices into one ritual and has given the Levites censer prerogatives which had formerly belonged only to the Aaronites. The narrative may well be an elaboration of events related in Ezra 6:17ff.; the genealogical insert (vss. 12-14) is a product of later times. These pro-Levitical traditions should be located early in the rise to power of the Levitical singers because the name, Asaph, is prominent precisely in this period.

E. Prophets to Levites

One short verse, 2 Chronicles 34:30, provides yet another clue to the purpose of the Chronicler. The problem is how to understand the seemingly insignificant change in one word. When we read the deuteronomistic history's account of Josiah's public reading of the law book, we find that among those listening were "the priests and the prophets" (2 Kgs 23:2). In Chronicles we find instead "the priests and the Levites" in the audience (2 Chr 34:30). An inadvertent slip? A change reflected by current practice? A textual error for which no other variants remain?

Most commentators have felt that cultic prophets, more specifically, Levitical singers, are intended by this "Levitical slip."[131] However, it is of course possible that the terminology of 2 Chr 35:18, "the priests and Levites," has influenced the wording of 2 Chr 34:30.

Since the change occurs in a relatively seamless narrative about the Josianic period, we can theorize that this terminological idiosyncracy was current with the basic Chronicler's narrative—correlative with Gese's IIIA. The fragmentary character of the issue dictates caution. However, I think that this one verse is an instance in which the Chronicler chose to identify the Levites of his own time with the prophets of Israel's past.

F. Josiah's Passover and Levitical Singers

Finally we come to a tantalizingly short reference to the tripartite division of the Levitical singers within the Chronicler's treatment of Josiah's Passover, 2 Chronicles 35:15. One of the major, if not the dominant, themes in this text is the stress on the importance of the Levitical function in the Passover proceedings.[132] Much has been written about the strange prescriptions for and nature of this Passover celebration.[133] Welch has argued that the passage is a confusing interweaving based on a redactor's attempt to make the original Chronicler's description consonant with the deuteronomistic practices, those described in Exodus and Numbers. According to Welch, at least parts of vss. 6, 12, 13, 14, 16 were the responsibility of a later redactor.[134]

> In this chapter, vs. 15 is particulary relevant to our study: The singers, the sons of Asaph, were functioning according to the command of David and Asaph and Heman, and Jeduthun, the king's seer; and the gatekeepers were at each and every gate. It was not necessary for them to cease their service, because their brethren the Levites prepared for them. (2 Chr 35:15)

This verse strikes a dissonant chord on several counts. The singular *ḥozeh* is unusual, ". . . Jeduthun the seer." If this reading were correct, we would have to understand Jeduthun as somehow superior to his two companions. However, we know of no stage in the singer traditions in which Jeduthun alone has elevated status. Consequently, the plural *hozê, supported by LXX, V, S, and T, has been suggested often. Nonetheless, following the MT reading, one may just as easily argue that the singular reading represents an earlier edition and that the phrase *kᵉmiṣwat . . . wîdutûn* was later inserted at the IIIA stage of development. The earlier document—reading "the sons of Asaph, the king's seer"—would represent the same traditio-historical stage as 2 Chronicles 29 where Asaph alone occurs as the seer.

A further problem occurs when we attempt to be precise about the meaning of the phrase, "their brethren the Levites." Are we to think that the singers are and the doorkeepers are not Levites? The Hebrew syntax implies that both singers and doorkeepers have the same relation to the Levites. If our suggestion about the existence of an earlier form of the text is correct, that Asaph was present without any other singers, then the conditions of that earlier edition must influence our understanding of the problem of the relationships between Levites, singers, and doorkeepers. The stage of Levitical singers traditions in which Asaph occurred alone was Gese's IIIA. And in this stage, neither the singers nor the doorkeepers were accounted as Levites. Consequently, vs. 15 preserves a description of the singers as non-Levitic even though it has included the IIIA description of the singer divisions, a revision prior to the dominant stress on the Korahites.

The best way to understand the identity of "the brethren" is to contend that vs. 15 is related to vs. 6 (which Welch has stated is a later interpolation), for it is in vs. 6 that the Levites are charged to take care of their "brethren." The specification of this group, the gatekeepers, comes in vs. 15.[135]

2 Chr 25:15 is therefore yet another example of the use of the prophetic title to give authority to the Levitical singers. The verse is a conflation of two traditio-historical stages: one in which Asaph, though not a Levite, was called "seer" and a second in which the two remaining singers, Heman and Jeduthun, were included so that they might receive the same honor as Asaph.

What then may one conclude on the basis of this study of the Chronicler's history? First, the Levitical singers were not cultic prophets in the monarchic period but were instead participants in the second temple ritual performance, the service of song. We also discovered, following the work of H. Gese, that the Levitical singers were not a homogenous group; Asaphites and Korahites were vying for ascendancy. Second, the Chronicler and his redactors have gone to great trouble to argue that the Levitical singers of Israel's past were really prophets and that their heritage is preserved by the Levitical singers of the second temple. The ways in which the Chronicler made this argument vary. He once changed one word so that the Levites would appear to be prophets (2 Chr 34:20). On one occasion he subtly worked with genealogies so that it would appear that David had appointed the Levitical singers as prophets (1 Chr 25). He also reconceptualized Israel's holy war so that Levitical prophets were understood to be crucial for Israel's success against her foes (2 Chr 20). And on another occasion, Levites and Levitical prophets were portrayed as better than priests and given special priestly prerogatives (2 Chr 29). Consistent in this variety is, however, the Chronicler's depiction of the Levitical singers as prophets. Prophecy was, for the Chronicler, an activity that could be performed in the second temple period by the Levitical singers.

[1]Welch has amply demonstrated the significance of prophecy for the Chronicler. A. Welch, *The Work of the Chronicler* (London: Oxford Univ., 1939) 42-54.

[2]After Samuel, the group includes: 1 Chronicles 17— Nathan to David, 1 Chronicles 21—Gad to David, 2 Chronicles 10—Ahijah to Jeroboam, 2 Chronicles 11—12—Shemaiah to Rehoboam, 2 Chronicles 15—Azariah ben Oded to Asa, 2 Chronicles 16—Hanani to Asa, 2 Chronicles 18—Micaiah ben Imlah to Ahab, 2 Chronicles 19—Jehu ben Hanani to Jehoshaphat, 2 Chronicles 20—Eliezer to Jehoshaphat, 2 Chronicles 21—Elijah to Jehoram, 2 Chronicles 24—prophets to the princes, 2 Chronicles 25:6-12—unnamed prophets to Amaziah, 2 Chronicles 28—Oded to Ahaz, 2 Chronicles 32—Isaiah to Hezekiah, 2 Chronicles 33—seers to Manasseh, 2 Chronicles 34—Huldah to Josiah, 2 Chronicles 36—Jeremiah to Zedekiah.

[3]As will become clear later, I do not understand Ezra and Nehemiah to be part of the original Chronicler's history but rather to be later additions, based on independent memoirs.

[4]See here W. Beuken, *Haggai-Sacharja 1—8. Studien zur Überlieferungsgeschichte der frühnachexilischen Prophetie* (SSN 10; Assen: Van Gorcum, 1967).

[5]For a differing view on eschatology in Chronicles, cf. W. Stinespring, "Eschatology in Chronicles," *JBL* 80 (1961) 209-219 and R. Mosis, *Untersuchungen zur Theologie des chronistischen Geschichtswerkes* (FTS 92; Freiburg; Herder, 1972).

[6]Plöger, *Theocracy and Eschatology* 38, W. Rudolph, *Chronikbücher* (HAT 21; Tübingen: J.C.B. Mohr, 1955) VIII.

[7]I make no claim for exhaustive treatment of the theme, "Prophecy in Chronicles." There are many reports of prophetic performance and speeches which parallel the deuteronomistic account. These deserve lengthy treatment; see provisionally C. Westermann, "Excursus: Prophetic Speeches in the Books of Chronicles," *Basic Forms of Prophetic Speech* (Philadelphia: Westminster, 1967) 163-168; and more recently J. Newsome, *The Chronicler's View of Prophecy* (Vanderbilt Ph.D. thesis, 1973) and *idem* "Toward a New Understanding of the Chronicler and His Purposes," *JBL* (1975) 210-212.

The many references to written prophetic records have also been studied by T. Willi. He has argued that these citations do not represent a prophetic strain in Chronicles (so Jepsen) nor do they constitute evidence of source material peculiar to Chronicles. Rather, they inform us about the traditio-historical perspective of the Chronicler. On the basis of close correlations between the deuteronomistic history and Chronicles, Willi concludes that Chronicles' prophetic citations function as interpretations of the deuteronomistic history. For the Chronicler, the prophetic history writers are understood as the primary historians: "God's action and word are one; what he says happens. And since the prophets have to do with his word which effects history, they are therefore entrusted as the first ones with the attested written record of the holy history as a basis of belief for those who come later," (cf. 2 Chr 26:22). T. Willi, *Die Chronik als Auslegung. Untersuchungen zur literarischen Gestaltung der historischen Überlieferung Israels* (FRLANT 106; Göttingen: Vandenhoeck & Ruprecht, 1972) 240.

[8]K. Galling, *Die Bücher der Chronik, Esra, Nehemiah* (ATD 12; Göttingen: Vandenhoeck & Ruprecht, 1954) 14-17.

[9]J. Myers, *Chronicles,* Vol 1 (AB 12; Garden City: Doubleday, 1965) LXIII.

[10]S. Japhet, "The Supposed Common Authorship of Chronicles and Ezra-Nehemiah," *VT* 18 (1968) 331-332.

[11]D. Freedman, "The Chronicler's Purpose," *CBQ* 23 (1961) 439-440 and T. Willi, *Die Chronik als Auslegung,* 176-184.

[12]Freedman, "The Chronicler's Purpose," 437.

[13]Two studies corroborating the thesis of a late sixth-century date for the basic Chronicler's history have appeared since these pages were first written. F. Cross, "A Reconstruction of the Judean Restoration," *JBL* 94 (1975) 4-18 (also appearing in *Interp* 29 [1975] 187-201) and J. Newsome "Toward a New Understanding of the Chronicler and His Purpose," *JBL* 94 (1975) 201-217.

[14]E. Bickerman, *From Ezra to the Last of the Maccabees. Foundations of Postbiblical Judaism* (New York: Schocken, 1962) 23-24.

[15]Both G. von Rad, *Das Geschichtsbild des chronistischen Werkes* (BWANT 4/3; Stuttgart: W. Kohlhammer, 1930) and Willi have demonstrated that the Chronicler depends upon the deuteronomistic history for his method and perspective.

[16]So J. Bright, *A History of Israel* (Philadelphia: Westminster, 1972) 310 and W. Rudolph, *Chronikbücher*, 315-317.

[17]P. Welten, *Geschichte und Geschichtsdarstellung in den Chronikbüchern* (WMANT 42; Neukirchen-Vluyn: Neukirchener Verlag, 1973) 199-200.

[18]Myers, *Chronicles*, LXIII.

[19]Galling, *Die Bücher der Chronik* 14-17.

[20]J. Rothstein and J. Hänel, *Kommentar zum ersten Buch der Chronik* (Leipzig: A. Deichert, 1927), Welch, *The Work of the Chronicler;* Rudolph has also rightly observed that the number of such insertions and/or redactions decreases in 2 Chronicles, *Chronikbücher* VIII.

[21]F. Cross, "A Reconstruction of the Judean Restoration," 11-14.

[22]See Welch, *The Work of the Chronicler* 55ff., Rudolph, *Chronikbücher* XV and *passim*, von Rad, *Das Geschichtsbild des chronistischen Werkes* 80ff.

[23]J. Köberle, *Die Tempelsänger im Alten Testament* (Erlangen: Verlag Fr. Junge, 1899) 182ff.

[24]von Rad, *Das Geschichtsbild*, 99-100.

[25]*Ibid.*, 107.

[26]*Ibid.*, 110-114.

[27]H. Gese, "Zur Geschichte der Kultsänger am zweiten Tempel," *Abraham unser Vater: Juden und Christen im Gespräch über die Bibel* (Leiden: F. J. Brill, 1963) 222-234.

[28]Gese's analysis yields the following chronology: I, before 515 B.C. or the last one third of the sixth century; II, middle of the fifth century; IIIA, second half of the fourth or towards the end of the fourth century; IIIB, the end of the fourth century or soon after 300. For the reasons stated above, this relative chronology should be revised upward.

[29]Buss' observation that the Asaphite psalms preserve Northern traditions while Korahite psalms evidence concern for Zion-Jerusalem is consistent with Gese's thesis about different singer traditions. M. Buss, "The Psalms of Asaph and Korah," *JBL* 82 (1963) 382-392.

[30] Gese, "Zur Geschichte," 223 and von Rad, *Das Geschichtsbild*, 113-114.

[31]This is not meant to deny that Johnson, Haldar, Jeremias, and many others, have done important work on the subject of cultic prophecy. It is simply to say that the seminal thesis of Levitical singers as cultic prophets was proposed by S. Mowinckel, *Psalmenstudien III. Kultprophetie und prophetische Psalmen* (Amsterdam: P. Schippers, 1961).

[32]Mowinckel also mentions 2 Chronicles 20 and 1 Chronicles 15, texts which will be considered later in this chapter.

[33]Mowinckel, *Kultprophetie* 22.

[34]LXX reads: *kai chōnenia archōn tōn leueitōn archōn tōn 'odōn*, "and Chonenia, head of the Levites, leader of music," omitting the first *bammaśśā⁾. yāsōr* is a problem. Is it an infinitive absolute from *ysr* or a *nomen agentis* as Rudolph, *Chronikbücher* 119 and *GK* #84k argue? Cf. Rothstein, *Kommentar zum ersten Buch der Chronik* 280. Some MSS read *yśr*, from *śrr*, "he will superintend." I favor the latter reading.

[35]*BDB* 672.

[36]So Rothstein on 1 Chronicles 15:17.

[37]von Rad, *Das Geschichtsbild* 110.

[38]Rothstein thinks *hamšōreʾrîm* is a later gloss. Following his excisions in vs. 22, we would be left with the same phrase in vs. 27. Bertheau's ingenious suggestion that *hamšōreʾrîm* is a corruption of *weḥaśśōᶜʾarîm* on the basis of confusion with *hammaśśā⁾* seems forced, Bertheau, *Die Bücher der Chronik*, cited in Rudolph, *Chronikbücher* 119.

[39]That what we have intended by *weśārê hassābā⁾* is not military leaders, but the leaders of the Levites has been clearly shown by E. Curtis, *The Books of Chronicles* (New York: Scribner's, 1910) 279 n. 1, though I do not accept Curtis' inclusion of *laᶜabōdāh* as a genitival description of this leadership.

[40]Rothstein's protestations against MT on the basis of LXX[B]*estēsen* appear groundless. Not only is the root, *bdl*, used in similar ways to mean "designate" or "appoint" but Rudolph has advanced the plausible thesis that *kai estēsen* is a scribal error for *diestēsen*, Rudolph, *Chronikbücher* 164.

[41]Most modern commentators are quick to adopt the *Qere, hannibbᵉᵓîm*, attested by LXX, V, and T, though MT makes good sense. To read a participle instead of a noun offers no significant change in meaning: *Ketib* "the prophets with . . ." versus *Qere* "who were to prophesy with. . . ." Rudolph recognizes the problem in his notes but finesses the solution in his translation, "who should practice proclamation with. . . ," avoiding the term "prophesy"; Rudolph, *Chronikbücher,* 164. Curtis cites vs. 2 *hannibbāᵓ* as evidence for a participial reading (actually vs. 3b is better for his argument). This form is not without its difficulties because there is textual evidence for a nominal reading; Curtis, *Chronicles* 279. Consequently one has to reckon with the possibility that a noun was also intended in vs. 1. The solution based solely on textual grounds is moot. The issue easily turns into an argument based on context. Were the singers, in the Chronicler's eye, performing prophetically prior to this order of the king? If one wants to stress the importance of the Davidic figure and initiative in Chronicles (as most commentators do), then the participial reading more closely fits this goal.

[42]Most commentators insert the name *šimᶜî* after Heshaiah on the basis of vs. 17. Without the name, which is included by LXX, we have only five singers, although the verse expressly states that there were six. To restore the text so quickly may lead one to ignore the question, why is the name missing? Is it a scribal mistake or do we have two different lists? (See below.)

[43]My translation is purposefully ambiguous. We might expect *lᵉhārîm qarnô* (reading *qarnô* instead of *qāren*) to mean another instrument allocated to the Heman group after the mention of other instruments. Though this interpretation has been proposed (T, Bertheau), there is an idiomatic usage which precludes such a reading. As Rudolph notes ". . . to raise or exalt the horn is to raise the fortunes of someone," (Rudolph, *Chronikbücher* 166 and Rothstein, *Der Chronik* 450); ". . . it is a sign of success or well-being," (Johnson, *The Cultic Prophet* [Cardiff: Univ. of Wales, 1962] 70 n. 3); cf. also 1 Sam 2:10; Deut 23:17; Lam 2:17; Pss 75:5; 89:18; 92:11; 112:9; 148:14. Clearly the numerical superiority of Heman's progeny is to be seen as a raising of his fortunes.

But then the exact sense of *bᵉdibrê hāᵓᵉlōhîm* is unclear within this context, if taken literally; for we have no record of a divine promise of progeny to Heman which could serve as the referent of this phrase. Rothstein and Ehrlich have both suggested that the phrase should be interpreted as "theological matters" (Rothstein) or "things of religion" (Ehrlich). The phrase thereby modifies the character of the seer's office — Heman advises the king in matters of religion. Rudolph, on the other hand, wants to see the words connected with the first part of the sentence and not in apposition to *hōzēh hammelek*. Consequently, he preserves the phrase, "words of God," as a promise, but does not clarify the nature of this unknown promise. I would prefer, with Ehrlich and Rothstein, to see the phrase related directly to the *hōzēh*. However, I should still insist on a more literal emphasis on the "words of God," especially since a prophetic title is here being used. This *dābār* terminology would further enhance the prophetic function. One might translate "seer of the king based upon the words of God," i.e. making explicit the authority of the prophet (*KB,* 104 #16); cf. for similar usages 1 Kgs. 13:5; Dan 10:12.

[44]LXX[BA] omit *laᶜᵃbōdat bêt hāᵓᵉlōhîm* and the verse reads more smoothly without this apparent insertion.

[45]J. Böhmer, "Sind einige Personennamen in 1 Chr 25:4 'kunstlich geschaffen'?" *BZ* 22 (1934) 93-100.

[46]P. Haupt, "Die Psalmenverse in 1 Chr 25:4," *ZAW* 34 (1914) 142-145.

[47]H. Torczyner, "A Psalm by the Sons of Heman," *JBL* 68 (1949) 247-249.

[48]Rothstein, *Kommentar zum ersten Buch der Chronik* 453, see below p. 67.

[49]At one time, I thought it might be possible to detect an Aramaic original behind this Hebrew hymnic fragment. One could argue for this on several grounds. (1) *hnny* could be an Aramaic form since ᶜ″ᶜ verbs may be identical to the strong verb morphology (F. Rosenthal, *A Grammar*

of Biblical Aramaic [Wiesbaden: Otto Harrassowitz, 1963], #157), though this usually happens only in the elevated stems. (2) The roots ⁾*th* and *mll* enjoy greater frequency in Aramaic than they do in Hebrew. (3) *rmmty* could be read as the not uncommon Aramaic *polel*. However, certain considerations make this Aramaic interpretation improbable. If the poem were originally Aramaic, we would not expect ᶜ*dr* and *yšb* (if one accepts the reading of Rudolph), though it should be noted that both ᶜ*dr* and *yšb* do occur in Aramaic inscriptions. Further, the last two cola are virtually impossible to interpret within the context of Aramaic morphology. Finally, both ⁾*th* and *mll* (or *ml*⁾ following Haupt) are used in BH. Perhaps the most one can say is that the piece possesses an Aramaic flavor consistent with a composition date in the Persian period.

⁵⁰Ehrlich, *Randglossen*, Vol. 7, 350.

⁵¹Gunkel and Begrich note that very similar phrases are to be found in the Babylonian psalm material (H. Gunkel and J. Begrich, *Einleitung in die Psalmen* [Göttingen: Vandenhoeck & Ruprecht, 1933] 220).

⁵²Cf. 2 Chr 35:21 for the term used in a martial sense which might not be foreign in a request for aid such as we find here. The apparent Deut 33:2, 21 parallel usages are still interesting even though Cross and Freedman have excised them from the earlier Yahwistic text (F. Cross and D. Freedman, "The Blessing of Moses," *JBL* 67 [1948] 191-210).

⁵³Reading the relative particle *š*. Cf. Ps 34:4 for the same verbs paired together.

⁵⁴Cf. 1 Chr 12:1. If we were correct in noting a military connotation in ⁾*th*, the use of ᶜ*zr* buttresses the martial idiom. Note H. Ginzburg's treatment of the term in Ugaritic and BH, "Ugaritic Parallel to 2 Sam 1:21," *JBL* 57 (1938) 210-211.

⁵⁵Cf. Esth 5:7, 8; 7:3 for this form of *bqš*. Note also the semantically identical *ml*⁾ *š*⁾*l* in Ps 20:6 and in Syriac (Haupt, "Die Psalmenverse in 1 Chr 25:4," 143).

⁵⁶Following Haupt, "Die Psalmenverse in 1 Chr 25:4," 143, a scribal error for *mlyty* = *ml*⁾*ty*.

⁵⁷Also with Haupt, a plural form equalling *mḥzywt* of singular *mḥzyt* which can be explained by analogy with singular *mškyt* and plural *mškywt* where we also find the form *mšky*⁾*t*.

⁵⁸Haupt *et al.* have argued that we should translate not "oracles" or "visions," but something like the Targum for Exod 3:3: *ḥzwnh rbh* (cf. BH *hmr*⁾*h hgdl*), "a noteworthy event or occurrence." This contention of Haupt's is predicated on the assumption that the nominal form, *mḥzyt*, may be equated with *ḥzwh* and hence with *mr*⁾*h*. However, there are other nominal forms from *ḥzh* which offer the alternative "vision," *mḥzh* to cite one. Haupt has simply opted for one semantic bundle which the two roots, *r*⁾*h* and *ḥzh*, share, when there is an equally legitimate and more probable bundle, "vision" or "oracle." Both these roots have nouns, *mr*⁾*h* and *mḥzt* to cite two, which are used very consciously to describe prophetic activity. In opposition to Haupt and Rudolph (*Chronikbücher* 167), the translation "oracle" or "vision" makes a good deal of sense.

⁵⁹See the form-critical matter, Rudolph, *Chronikbücher* 167; Eissfeldt, *The Old Testament. An Introduction.* (Oxford: Blackwell, 1965) 115ff.

⁶⁰Rudolph, *Chronikbücher* 168.

⁶¹B. Gemser, *De Beteekenis der Persoonsnamen voor onze Kennis van Het Leven en Denken der oude Babyloniërs en Assyriers* (Wageningen: H. Veenman & Zone, 1924) 22.

⁶²Welch, *The Work of the Chronicler* 90.

⁶³Curtis, *Chronicles* 276.

⁶⁴Rothstein, *Kommentar* 453.

⁶⁵Notes to 1 Chr 25:2-4a and 9-31:

Some of the names are the same: *zakkôr, yôsēp, gᵉdalyāhû, būqqiyyāhû, yišaᶜîyhû, mattanyāhû*. Then there are three cases in which we may note minor orthographic differences: vs. 22 *yīrēmôt* parallel to vs. 4 *yīrîmôt* reflect the same vowel, while vs. 2 *nᵉtanyāh* parallel to vs. 12 *nᵉtanyāhû* and vs. 3 *ḥᵃšabyāhû* parallel to vs. 19 *ḥᵃšabyāh* simply reflect the orthographic possibilities of rendering the theophoric element *yāh/yāhû*. The other differences are more complex. (1) Vs. 2 ⁾ᵃ*śar*⁾*ēlāh* parallel to vs. 14 *yiśar*⁾*ēlah* is especially difficult. Noth has suggested that the primary form is to be found in vs. 2 and is to be connected with the Arabic *ašira* and to be translated "God has filled with joy" (M. Noth, *Die israelitischen Personennamen im Rahmen der gemeinsemitischen Namengebung* [Stuttgart: W. Kohlhammer, 1928] 183). Rothstein, on the other hand, wants to see vs. 14 as primary, being an altered form of *yiśra*ᵓ*ēl*. The versions are ambiguous, though there is some evidence that LXX translators read a form without a *r*. The versions (LXX and V) are more uniform with *y*ᵉ*śer*ᵓ*ēlah*. I think it is easier to explain the existence of the two forms if one sees ᵓ*śr*ᵓ*lh* as a product of an early misreading of ᵓ for *y*. Noth's attempt to explain the form on the basis of *š* ignores the present textual variants. (2) Vs. 3 *ṣ*ᵉ*rî* parallel to vs. 11 *yiṣrî* is another problem. The respective presence and absence of the *y* is supported by the versions: The question is: can we argue that *ṣ*ᵉ*rî* is an apocopated form of *yiṣrî*, itself short for *yṣryhw*, "God created?" Rudolph says the issue is moot. However, since *ṣ*ᵒ*rî*, "balsam," is never used as a proper name and since *yṣr* is not unknown to Hebrew names, probability would rest with interpreting *ṣ*ᵉ*rî* as derivative of *yiṣrî*. Noth asserts that the converse is the case, that *ṣ*ᵉ*rî* has been expanded to *yiṣrî;* though probability is against such a move (Noth, *Die israelitischen Personennamen* 247). (3) The presence of *šim*ᶜ*î* in vs. 17 and its absence in vs. 3 where it is needed to make up the progeny of six can be explained (following Rudolph) by haplography due to the similarity of the preceding word; so also with LXX^(BA) and V. Again it should be noted that, copyist mistake or no, the fuller list is preserved in vss. 9-31. (4) The names ᶜ*ūzî*ᵓ*ēl* (vs. 4) and ᶜᵃ*zarēl* (vs. 18) create a problem because both may stand as legitimate North-West Semitic names: "El is my strength" and "El helped." One could argue that either *r* or *y* could have been misread for the other, but it is impossible to ascertain which way the error would have progressed. I would prefer to see *r > y* but it is mere preference. Many commentators (e.g. Rudolph, *Chronikbücher* 166) have pointed to the possibility that we have a similar case as with the Judahite king name, ᶜ*ūziyyāhû* or ᶜᵃ*zaryāh*. But one has to ask, what sort of similar case? Are we to understand the differences in the king's names as orthographic variants or the difference between regnal and personal names? Following Honeyman and Albright, I would argue that the Uzziah/Azariah differences are bound up in the traditio-historical assimilations of the regnal versus personal names within Israel's historical documents. (A. Honeyman, "The Evidence for Regnal Names among the Hebrews," *JBL* 67 [1948] 13ff.; W. F. Albright, "The Chronology of the Divided Monarchy in Israel," *BASOR* 100 [1945] 16-22.) And this is surely not the case in the Chronicles passages. (5) The *š*ᵉ*bû*ᵓ*ēl* of vs. 4 (and also 1 Chr 23:16 and 1 Chr 26:24) most probably reflects a misreading from *šubā*ᵓ*ēl* in vs. 20 (following Noth, *Die israelitischen Personennamen* 257). The versions support this analysis since LXX^B reads *Soubaēl* and V, *Subuel*, in vs. 4.

⁶⁶Gese, "Der Kultsänger," 227.

⁶⁷Reading Ammonites, again, makes little sense, cf. 2 Chr 26:7. As Curtis notes (*Chronicles* 405), three groups of people are presumed in vss. 10, 22, 24. The LXX^(BA) reading *mēhamm*ᵉᶜ*ûnîm*, is to be preferred.

⁶⁸Though there is a manuscript which reads *mē*ᵓᵉ*dôm*, this correction could also be made on the basis of suggesting a misreading of *d* to *r*. S and Ethiopic read "Red Sea," *ym* ᵓ*dm*.

⁶⁹*š*ᵉ*pôṭ*, infinitive construct, does not read easily here. Ehrlich suggests *šôṭ* as in Job 9:23. However, an explanation based upon a metathesis of *ṭ* and *p* seems more satisfactory, thus giving us *šepeṭ*, "flood."

⁷⁰Restore the *l* before *p*ᵉ*nê*. Omission due to haplography because of *l* at the end of *hannahal*.

⁷¹Though Ehrlich's suggestion that *hityaṣṣ*ᵉ*bû* be translated "notice" or "pay attention" is not without merit, (cf. 1 Sam 12:16) the context would seem to favor a more military connotation, as in Jer 46:4.

⁷²Reading *waw explicativum* (. . . *wmt*) as Gese, Galling and Rudolph have suggested. Cf. *GK* #154a n. 1 (b).

⁷³After examination of the other occurrences of *l*ᵉ*hadrat qōdeš* (1 Chr 16:29; Ps 29:2; 96:9), we may reject Ehrlich's suggestion that the phrase is to be read "for the beautification of holy action."

⁷⁴Quite apart from the difficulties such a solution raises, Ehrlich's proposal that we read ᶜ*bb* "to mix" and here "confusion," on the basis of a Mishnaic text, ignores the obvious battle imagery present in *m*ᵉᵓ*ār*ᵉ*bîm*.

⁷⁵Rudolph's attempt to get rid of the ironic tone of the help by reading a *polal*, ᶜ*wrrw*, based on T might be defended if ᶜ*az*ᵉ*rû* made no sense *(Chronikbücher*, 262). However, the semantic range of ᶜ*zr* is larger than Boy-Scout type aid (cf. Zech 1:15).

[76]Reading *bᵉhēmāh* with LXX.

[77]Several Hebrew manuscripts and one Vulgate text probably present us with the original reading, *ûbᵉgādîm*, though probably as the result of a correction and not on the basis of some textual tradition. LXX glossed the issue and translated *skula*, "booty."

[78]Omit *lašōb* following LXX^BA, though not *ᵓel-yᵉrûšālayim*. The double use of the verb is redundant.

[79]On Seir, see Welten *Geschichte und Geschichtsdarstellung* 144-145.

[80]J. Wellhausen, *Prolegomena to the History of Ancient Israel* (New York: World Publishing Co., 1957) 208.

[81]M. Noth, "Eine palästinische Lokalüberlieferung in 2 Chr 20," *ZDPV* 67 (1945) 52. Cf. also Welten, *Geschichte und Geschichtsdarstellung* 148-149.

[82]Noth, "Eine palästinische Lokalüberlieferung," 60-71.

[83]*Ibid.*, 48.

[84]Rudolph, *Chronikbücher* 259.

[85]Myers, *Chronicles* Vol 2 114-115.

[86]Welten, *Geschichte und Geschichtsdarstellung* 153.

[87]Cf. Welten, *Ibid.*

[88]The fact that there are speeches is in and of itself significant. Plöger has argued that speeches are devices used by both the Deuteronomist and the Chronicler to emphasize specific historical events. The frequent use of prayers by the Chronicler (especially 1 Chr 29:10ff.; 2 Chr 20:6ff.; Ezra 9:6ff.) distinguishes his use of this literary device from the Deuteronomist and, most probably, reflects the liturgical practice of his time. (O. Plöger, "Reden und Gebete im deuteronomistischen und chronistischen Geschichtswerk," *Aus der Spätzeit des Alten Testaments* [Göttingen: Vandenhoeck & Ruprecht, 1971] 50-66.) On 2 Chronicles 20, see pp. 61-64.

[89]Eissfeldt, *The Old Testament* 112.

[90]W. Thrall and A. Hibbard, *A Handbook to Literature* (New York: Odyssey Press, 1960) 416.

[91]S. Mowinckel, "The 'Spirit' and the 'Word' in the Pre-Exilic Reforming Prophets," *JBL* 53 (1934) 199-227.

[92]Gese, "Der Kultsänger" 230 n. 2.

[93]Gese, "Der Kultsänger" 230.

[94]J. Begrich, "Das priesterliche Heilsorakel," *ZAW* 52 (1934) 82ff.

[95]Welten, *Geschichte und Geschichtsdarstellung* 148-150.

[96]I should not want to press this point too far, for as von Rad has noted, in certain instances, a rite of penance and public lacrimation may be a part of the holy war preparation (G. von Rad, *Der Heilige Krieg im alten Israel* [Göttingen: Vandenhoeck & Ruprecht, 1969] 7). However, in the usual pattern, we hear very little about such a ceremony. And since we know that such laments were enacted in times other than the holy war, there seems to be some justification in viewing it as a separate entity, at least for the purposes of analysis.

[97]G. von Rad, "The Levitical Sermon in I and II Chronicles," *The Problem of the Hexateuch and other Essays* (New York: McGraw-Hill, 1966) 273.

[98]G. von Rad, *Der Heilige Krieg* 9.

[99]*Ibid.*

[100]von Rad, "The Levitical Sermon" 274; Noth, "Eine palästinische Lokalüberlieferung" 47 note 1. Such dependence is difficult to prove since this language is common to other Hebrew Bible accounts (e.g. Exod 14ff.).

[101]Gese contends that the basic interest of the writer is in the activity of the singers, and more specifically, in the effect of the holy son ("Der Kultsänger" 231).

[102]von Rad, *Der Heilige Krieg* 11.

[103]*Ibid.* 81.

[104]Gese, "Der Kultsänger" 232-233.

[105]*Ibid.* 234.

[106]Plöger, "Reden und Gebete" *passim.*

[107]LXX[BA] reads "and it happened when he was over his kingdom in the first month," probably a paraphrastic rendition of MT.

[108]A broad plaza apparently near the city gate, and therefore not the temple court. Cf. Neh 8:1, 3; 2 Chr 32:6; Job 29:2. (Myers, *Chronicles* 168; Curtis, *Chronicles* 463; Rudolph, *Chronikbücher* 292.)

[109]The Hebrew at the end of vs. 9 and at the beginning of vs. 10 reads *baššᵉbî ʿal zōʾt ʿattāh*, ". . . in captivity because of this now . . ." LXX has been somewhat free and read *ʿattāh* as a part of vs. 9, "and thus it is now," i.e. they are still in captivity. I take this to be a legitimate reading of the Hebrew, though an interpretation based on the historical circumstances of the LXX translator. The style of this speech with its repeated use of *ʿattāh* (cf. vss. 5, 10, 11) suggests that *ʿattāh* should begin vs. 10.

[110]Ehrlich's proposal to read *bidbar* instead of *bᵉdibrê*, ʾssuming error by dittography of *y*, allows for easier reading.

[111]Rudolph has given the most convincing interpretation for the LXX[B] replacement of the number 16 by 13 as well as several other minor changes: "LXX[B] changes the sixteen days to thirteen. Thereby the cleansing work would be finished before the beginning of *Pesaḥ*, since the translator noticed that the usual dates did not correspond. At the beginning of the verses, *hēmera tē tritē* was placed between *tē* and *noumēnia* as a correction (5+8=13), then *tritē* in LXX[B] as replaced by *prōtē* so that *noumēnia* now exists superfluously" (Rudolph, *Chronikbücher* 294).

[112]The translation of *bᵉyad yhwh* is difficult. There is no parallel usage in the Old Testament which denotes a similar sort of mediation. The phrase is most often used literally (e.g. Exod 16:3; Jer 51:7; 1 Chr 21:13). Most modern commentators have attempted to read the phrase in a way designed to indicate agency (Galling, ". . . because the commandment was issued by the Lord, mediated by his prophets," *Die Bücher der Chronik* 155; Myers, ". . . for such was the command of Yahweh through his prophets," *Chronicles* 167). According to Rudolph, "*bᵉyad yhwh* is obviously an induced disturbance of *bᵉdawîd hāyāh* because of the second *bᵉyad* . . . ; the Peshitta and Arabic versions also speak of David in vs. 25b. Vs. 25b wants to explain why, in vs. 25a, the two prophets were appended to David." I think that neither the textual evidence nor the argument based on the supposed intention of vs. 25b are strong enough to warrant this change. The Chronicler appears less interested in the figure of David as such than he is in gaining authority for the Levites. Consequently, I would opt for a literal translation (so also Mitchell, *Chronicles* 468). The verse emphasizes not only that Yahweh was the source of the mediated message, but also that the prophets have mediated the message—down to and including the present Levitical prophets, i.e. through Asaph and his lineage.

[113]*wᵉʿal yᵉdê* denotes agency here as shown by LXX *pros*.

[114]There is an idiom, "to fill the hands" which is most often used to denote the consecration of ordination into the Aaronide priesthood. However, to charge that in this passage the addressee of vs. 31a is the priesthood on the basis of this idiomatic usage is to overlook both the obvious sense of vs. 31b (which is exceedingly difficult to separate from the first part of the verse) and to ignore two passages (Exod 32:29 and 1 Chr 29:5) in which this idiom requires a more reflexive translation. The Exodus passage, an enigmatic and probably corrupt text, presents Moses as saying either "Fill your hands" or "You filled your hands," i.e. qal imperative or piel perfect, and most probably the latter. This holy and intra-family slaughter is hardly to be thought of as a paradigmatic priestly investiture. Rather we have a reflexive use of the idiom, "to devote oneself." So also with 1 Chr 29:5 where, on appeal from Hezekiah, the citizens devote themselves to the Lord by giving up gold for the building of the temple. Consequently, it is difficult to follow the assertion of Myers that as a ". . . technical term for the consecration of priests . . . Hezekiah was addressing the priests exhorting them to carry on their functions now that the temple was dedicated" (Myers, *Chronicles* 169).

Rudolph's solution is a bit more complicated. Also recognizing the priestly consecration idiom, Rudolph feels that the priests must be the addressees. But he further argues: (1) there was no priestly dedication in the narrative; and (2) in vss. 31a and b the people are addressed, and the speech can not change in the middle of the sentence, something Myers has overlooked. He notes

Ehrlich's suggestion of *ml⁾ ⁾tm* (cf. 1 Chr 29:5): ". . . the insertion of *lᶜm* after *wy⁾mr*, which either intentionally fell out (in the jump from ᶜ to ᶜ and the deletion of the then unmeaningful *l*), or, after the reading mistake *ml⁾tm* had entered, they were omitted as unsuitable" (Rudolph, *Chronikbücher* 298). The reconstructed text of Ehrlich and Rudolph would read *wymr lᶜm ᶜth ml⁾ ⁾tm ydkm.*

This solution is interesting. The insertion of *lᶜm*, though the sense requires a noun, is not textually attested. Nor is the division of *ml⁾ ⁾tm.* We may understand this verse, I think, equally well if we understand the sense to be one of self-dedication, as in the Exodus passage. The meaning of the verse remains the same, whether my solution or that of Ehrlich and Rudolph is adopted.

[115]The use of the word "covenant" is intriguing, the more so since we find no other notice of a covenant ceremony in the description in Hezekiah's reign. However, the term is not inconsistent with the Chronicler's way of describing kings and covenants. For example, in 2 Chr 15:12; 23:16; and 34:31, we find Asa, Jehoida, and Josiah described as having made covenants as a part of a program to cleanse the cult from foreign influence; this is most probably also the case in 2 Chronicles 29.

[116]The dual use of the root *šrt* is puzzling. Welch contends that this ministry ". . . is the dignity which the law denied to the Levite and reserved to the priest" (Welch, *The Work of the Chronicler* 104). Though he is correct in seeing that the P tradition describes the function of the Aaronide priesthood with *šrt*, this P terminological usage hardly excludes the Levites. We often find the statement made that the Levite shall minister to the High Priest (Num 3:6; 8:26; 18:2). But other passages are less clear in their limitation of the Levitical service (Num 8:23ff.; 16:9). Furthermore, once we turn to the Deuteronomistic traditions, which are closely related to those of the Chronicler, the sense of the *šrt* language is more general and clearly not intended to separate Levitical service from that of the priests. The writer of vs. 11 in 2 Chronicles 29 most probably did not give the Levites a function they had not previously held.

[117]Cf. R. deVaux, *Ancient Israel: Religious Institutions* (New York: McGraw Hill, 1965) 422-423.

[118]M. Haran, "The Use of Incense in the Ancient Israelite Ritual," *VT* 10 (1960) 113-125. An incense altar has been found in the Arad sanctuary, Y. Aharoni, "Arad: Its Inscription and Temple," *BA* 31 (1968) 19.

[119]Cf. Ezek 44:10-13 for an attitude similar to the P redactor and against which the Chronicler was writing.

[120]K. Möhlenbrink, "Die levitischen Überlieferungen des Alten Testaments," *ZAW* 11 (1934) 230ff.

[121]There has been some debate about the status of vs. 19. Welch thinks it is an intrusion, as are the words *bᵉdibrê yhwh* in vs. 15, since, he argues, there was a basic document emphasizing the Levitic interests which later suffered a priestly redaction (Welch, *The Work of the Chronicler* 105). Others have contended quite the opposite, that vs. 19 represents one of the few original parts of the narrative, emphasizing the role of the priests. I think the latter is a more convincing position.

[122]Myers, *Chronicles*, Vol. 2, 171-172.

[123]J. Hänel, "Das Recht des Opferschlachtens in der chronistischen Literatur," *ZAW* 14 (1937) 47ff. See further on the nature of the burnt offering: W. Stevenson, "Hebrew ᶜolah and zebach Sacrifices," *Festschrift für Alfred Bertholet* (Tübingen: J. C. B. Mohr, 1950), 488-497, L. Rost, "Erwägungen zum israelitischen Brandopfer," *Von Ugarit nach Qumran* (Berlin: A. Töpelman, 1961) 177-183.

[124]The same emphasis on the identification of the Aaronites that we found in 2 Chron 29:21a is present in Lev 1:4. It should be noted that there is a tradition contrary to lay slaughter, that of the Levitical slaying of the animals (Ezek 44:11).

[125]Welch, *The Work of the Chronicler* 105.

[126]Rudolph, *Chronikbücher* 293.

[127]See above, and cf. Haag's attempt to see this distinction reflect the difference between

nomadic versus sedentary influences in the early monarchy (H. Haag, "Gad und Nathan," *Arachäologie und Altes Testament* (Tübingen: J. C. B. Mohr, 1970) 135-143.

[128]Rudolph, *Chronikbücher* 297-298.

[129]Rudolph, *Chronikbücher* 298-299.

[130]Welch equivocates and then says such an anti-priestly tone would be consistent with the original pro-levitic document (*The Work of the Chronicler*, 107-108).

[131]So Myers, *Chronicles,* Vol. 2, 208; von Rad, *Das Geschichtsbild* 114; Johnson, *The Cultic Prophet* 72; Galling, *Die Bücher der Chronik* 176.

[132]So with Rudolph, *Chronikbücher* 325; Curtis, *Chronicles* 515; I. Benzinger, *Die Bücher der Chronik* (Tübingen: J. C. B. Mohr, 1901) 131.

[133]The best two treatments are: Hänel, "Das Recht des Opferschlachtens" 49ff.; and Welch, *The Work of the Chronicler* 138ff., for a redaction-critical approach.

[134]Welch, *The Work of the Chronicler* 139ff.

I have great difficulty with the sections which describe the uncertain nature of the animal sacrifices. Why do the bulls, oiginally designated as paschal offerings (vs. 7) end up as burnt offerings (vs. 12) following MT *labbāqār*? One is sorely tempted to adopt *labbōqer* with Syriac and LXX[BA] and see a time description as we have with *ᶜd-lylh* in vs. 14 (cf. 1 Chr 9:27; 16:40; 2 Chr 2:3). Why are *šᵉlamîm* included at all; and why are they, when included, not prepared according to the normal Passover regulations? These perhaps unanswerable questions indicate the enigmatic character of this narrative.

[135]Welch suggested, wrongly, that these "brethren" are either the worshippers in vs. 5 or the priests in vss. 10ff. (Welch, *The Work of the Chronicler* 140).

Chapter IV

Conclusions

Israelite society underwent severe restructuring after the defeat of 587 B. C.
The community was fractured; some Israelites were taken in exile to Babylon,
others went to Egypt, while a sizeable group remained in Palestine.
Furthermore, governance in the community was disrupted; the Davidic line
no longer exerted control over all worshippers of Yahweh. That the exiled
Jehoiachin, though he remained the source of hope for restoration, had
significant power over his fellow countrymen in Babylon is doubtful.
Concomitant with these disruptions in Israelite life, classical prophets also
disappear from the scene. Jeremiah and Ezekiel are the last in the line of
classical prophets. As suggested earlier, the reasons for the demise of classical
prophecy are several. The crisis in authority as reflected in Jeremiah's
confrontations with other Yahwistic prophets made the prophet's task
difficult. Perhaps more importantly, after Jeremiah and Ezekiel, the
traditional loci for prophetic performance had disappeared. The close
association between prophet and the institutions of the monarchy was no
longer possible. Hence prophecy, as it had been understood from the time of
Amos, ceased. Haggai and Zechariah constitute an exception to this thesis.
However, once we realize that these two prophets were working assiduously
for the restoration of the temple community under the auspices of a Davidide
on the throne, we may understand them to be a last gasp of classical prophecy.

Building upon the analyses of Plöger, Steck, and Hanson, I have argued
that there was an essential bifurcation within post-exilic Israelite society, an
ideological split which is represented, on the one hand, by the Chronicler's
history, a work written and redacted by the Levitical members of the
Jerusalemite hierocracy, and on the other hand, by the deutero-prophetic
corpus (the label admittedly covers material more varied than that of the
Chronicler), literature composed by traditionists who preserved and added to
the oracles and narratives of Israel's classical prophets. This monograph has
analyzed the contrasting assessments of Israelite prophecy as represented in
the two aforementioned literatures.

Beginning with the deutero-Isaianic literature, the conception of the
prophetic office began to shift significantly. The author of this lyric-dramatic

poetry no longer claimed to be a prophet as had earlier, classical prophets. Rather, the task of being a prophet was thrust upon other persons or groups, e.g. Zion or a servant. Furthermore, prophecy gained a future connotation; it was something expected rather than a contemporary practice. Just as the poet expected a glorious new Exodus and a mighty new Jerusalem, so he looked forward to the reinstitution of earlier Israelite social structures, including kingship and prophecy, albeit in revised form (so the democratized Davidic throne, Isa 55:1-5).

Later deutero-prophetic writers denigrated attempts at prophetic activity during their own time, and instead, expected the return of prophecy as a part of a final, eschatological drama initiated by Yahweh. The return of prophecy was viewed in two ways: as a distribution of prophetic gifts to all true Yahwists and as the return of a prophet who was to prepare the true Yahwists for survival through the apocalyptic terror.

i

We are now in a position to ask and answer two important questions, the first of which is: why did the prophetic traditionists inveigh against prophecy in their own time? To be sure, the issue of false prophecy is one part of the answer. The book of Jeremiah attests to the serious credibility problem which sixth century prophets had in validating their oracles. Prophets in Israel could not speak with an automatically authoritative voice because the prophetic enterprise now suffered from an inherent crisis of authority. Hence any claim for prophetic powers or abilities was immediately suspect and liable to be polemicized by the prophetic traditionists.

Other grounds for the anti-prophetic element are illustrated by a comparison of Chronicles with the deutero-prophetic literature. As Hanson has recently noted, there was a basic antipathy between the visionary and the realist positions in at least two areas.[1] The hierocratic authorities were willing to collaborate with the Persians whereas the prophetic traditionists were content to wait for Yahweh to act without foreign partners sullying Israel's hands. Second, the absence of any eschatological dimension in Chronicles demonstrates the ideological chasm between the two groups. The prophetic traditionists were expecting a radical change in the future whereas the hierocrats were satisfied with the status quo.

The most important reason for the anti-prophetic polemic raised by the prophetic traditionists, however, depends upon the specific group, the Levitical prophets, which this monograph has studied in some detail. At approximately the same time the deutero-prophetic literature was being written, the Chronicler's history was composed and redacted. Fortunately this history preserves certain developments and procedures in the official cult from the Chronicler's own time. One such striking development was the depiction of the Levitical singers as prophets. The singers of David's time were labelled in the same fashion as were the court prophets Gad and Nathan.

Furthermore, Levitical singers throughout Israelite history were often described as having performed classical prophetic functions. Even the essential work of the singers, the cultic song, was, according to the Chronicler, prophetic performance.

Though this claim for prophetic authority was made by certain Asaphites and Korahites in order to achieve greater prestige within the cult, the ramifications of that claim reached beyond the cult. The impact of the claim that the Levitical singers were cultic prophets upon the prophetic traditionists was profound. Had this claim of the Levites been empty verbiage the deutero-prophetic writers might have been able to ignore it. However, three features of the post-exilic cult provided grounds for a dispute over the possibility of prophetic activity in that time. First, the singers' essential function was vocal participation in the cult, chanting liturgies, the words for some of which are preserved in the Psalter. It is well known from the study of Israel's psalms that certain cultic procedures were often typologically similar to prophetic performance, i.e. a holy man spoke on behalf of Yahweh. Such was the priestly role in giving an oracle of assurance to the supplicant in a lament ceremony. If being a prophet meant speaking Yahweh's word, then such cultic performance might have easily been viewed as prophetic. If the Levites were engaged in this cultic activity their claim to be Yahweh's prophets would have been all too clear to the prophetic traditionists.

Second, in the post-exilic period, a group of psalms were attributed to the temple singers. No longer were they considered to be anonymous songs or poems implicitly ascribed to David; they were now ascribed to identifiable individuals, just as prophetic words were attributed to specific persons. These songs comprise the Korahite group (42-49; 84-88) and the Asaphite collection (50; 73-83).[2] Strikingly the individuals who are viewed as authors of these collections are the same singers which the Chronicler depicts as prophets. From the perspective of the Chronicler, the psalms just mentioned would have been, by definition, a prophetic corpus, words, perhaps even oracles, attributable to Israel's prophets. Such a claim based on the Chronicler's ideology would have been a direct threat to the conception of an authoritative collection of classical prophetic words held by the prophetic traditionists. For this reason, too, the deutero-prophetic writers inveighed against prophecy in their own time.

A final ground for deutero-prophetic invective derives from the particular psalms attributed to the Chronicler's Levitical prophets. Not only were the Asaphites and then the Korahites claiming to be prophets, but their cultic activity suggested that they even attempted to perform like prophets—by using prophetic material in their songs.[3] As Buss notes, ". . . the Levitical psalms almost monopolize the direct use of oracles."[4] If second temple psalm singers and writers were using prophetic material, and were being called prophets by the Chronicler, then it is no wonder that the prophetic traditionists would have polemicized all attempts at prophetic activity. The traditionists were concerned to preserve the authority of earlier prophets' words since these words provided the basis for their exegetical reflection and devotion.

There is strong evidence of "prophetic" activity by the singers. We noticed an absence of the prophetic "I" in the deutero-prophetic literature. In contrast, the "I" becomes an identifying mark of certain psalms. As Buss says, "The presence of so-called prophetic psalms inhe Psalter is thus by no means an anomaly. On the contrary, it is these and other songs that represent the musicians', the Levitical singers', own psalms. In these, the first-person singular pronoun refers to the singer himself. . . ."[5] In the classical prophetic literature, the "I" had referred to the prophet himself. Because of the appropriation of the title, "prophet," and other definitive features of classical prophecy, like the singers' use of the prophetic "I," the prophetic traditionists had good reason to suspect that the Levitical singers were attempting to gain prophetic authority. Hence they adopted a posture designed to protect the past ideal of classical prophecy from spurious encroachment in the present; they argued that prophecy was a thing of the past and to be expected only in the future.

ii

The second important question which we must address is: what impact upon later traditions about prophecy did the late sixth and early fifth century developments which we have examined here have? Attempts to create a form of post-exilic cultic prophecy by the Asaphite and Korahite singers were ultimately unsuccessful.[6] Whether the polemic by the prophetic traditionists or the power of the Zadokites in the cultic establishment was more important in quashing these attempts, we will probably never know. Prophetic performance in the classical sense did not belong to the second temple cultus. Hence this period was known as a time in which prophecy had passed from the scene. Numerous texts attest to this fact: Ps 74:9—"there is no longer any prophet;" 1 Mac 9:27—"thus there was great distress in Israel, such as had not been since the time that prophets ceased to appear among them;" the survey of famous men in Sir 49:10; Josephus' comment, "because of the failure of the exact succession of the prophets" (Ap i. 41); and the tradition complex in the New Testament which speaks of the violent fate of the prophets (Matt 5:11ff.; 23:29-36; Luke 6:22ff.; 11:47-51; 13:31-33).[7] Therefore, only one side of the early exilic debate over prophecy remained alive, that of the deutero-prophetic writers who held that prophecy was a thing of the past and would only return immediately before Yahweh acted mightily on Israel's behalf.

In the Greco-Roman era, the unexpected return of prophecy was a hope which reflected precisely the program of the deutero-prophetic writers.[8] One major configuration of the tradition was the return of prophecy to all true Yahwists. Israel was to become a prophetic people by the pouring out of Yahweh's spirit when the new age arrived. The prophetic phenomena in the

Lucan infancy narrative surely reflect this expectation: "Zechariah 'prophesied' (1:67), Simeon was subject to revelation by the Holy Spirit (2:25-27), and Anna was a "prophetess" (2:36).[9] This same basic tradition of a universal prophetic gift may be observed in early Chrisitian reflection on Pentecost with the appropriation of Joel 3:1-5 into Acts 2, an exegetical maneuver which helped the early Christian community understand the significance of that "mighty wind."

The other lineal descendent of deutero-prophetic expectations about the return of prophecy in the Greco-Roman period is the tradition of the eschatological prophet.[10] 1 Macc 4:46 preserves this expectation: "(and they) stored the stones in a convenient place on the temple hill until there should come a prophet to tell them what to do with them."[11] Two exceedingly important texts from Qumran also allude to a prophetic figure prior to the coming of the Messiah.[12] 4QTest begins by juxtaposing two passages from Deuteronomy (5:28-29; 18:18-19). The emphasis appears to rest on the latter text: "I will raise up for them a prophet like you from among their brethren. . . ." Following this text are two more quotations from the Old Testament intended to foretell the appearance of two other coming figures: the royal (Num 24:15-17)˙ and the priestly (Deut 33:8-11) Messiahs (concluding the Testimonia is a section from the Psalms of Joshua). In this context, the prophet is apparently an individual who is to appear before the Messianic figures arrive.

A more specific statement of this expectation is made in the Community Rule. IQS 9:11 speaks about the prophet who shall come: "They shall depart from none of the counsels of the Law to walk in the stubbornness of their hearts, but shall be ruled by the primitive precepts in which the men of the Community were first instructed until there shall come the prophet and the Messiahs of Aaron and Israel." That the prophet was indeed a precursor and not a royal or Messianic figure is certain, since as Brown noted, there is no place at the eschatological banquet for the prophet.[13]

Starcky has published an Aramaic translation of Mal 3:23 (4Q Messar) which, he contends, shows that Elijah was thought to be the eschatological prophet by the community at Qumran.[14] There is, however, no other evidence that Elijah was designated as the precursor prophet. Rather it seems that the expectations of a Moses and an Elijah figure had merged. As Vermes says:

> The figure of the Prophet probably evolved from two biblical sources, the first being Deut 18:18-19, where Moses announces the coming of a Prophet similar to himself. . . , and the second being Mal 4:5, where it is prophesied that Elijah will return before the coming of the day of the Lord.[15]

The teacher of righteousness complicates the picture of the eschatological˙ prophet at Qumran since he appears to have certain prophetic qualities. Some scholars have sought to identify the teacher of righteousness with the eschatological prophet.[16] Following Brown, I am more inclined to think that the teacher of righteousness achieved a quasi-prophetic status because he was an interpreter of prophetic words. For example, the following description appears in IQpHab, ". . . the Teacher of Righteousness, to whom God made known all the mysteries of the words of His servants the Prophets."[17] He is never referred to as the precursor or eschatological prophet because he died before the last times; CD 9:29 suggests that there was to be a hiatus between the death of the teacher of righteousness and the coming Messiahs.[18] The eschatological prophet constituted part of the community's expectation for the age to come.

In the New Testament, the tradition of the eschatological prophet was still very much alive.[19] More than one person was looked on as the expected prophet. John the Baptist was judged to be a prophet (Matt 14:5; 21:26), and even more, was considered to be the eschatological prophet, "He is Elijah who is to come" (Matt 11:14.)[20]

Jesus, too, was accorded prophetic status, sometimes as Elijah redivivus and sometimes as the expected new Moses.[21] Matt 16:13b-14 depicts this expectation:

> Jesus asked his disciples, "Who do you say that the Son of man is?" And they said, "Some say John the Baptist, others say Elijah, and others Jeremiah or one of the prophets."

Pursuing the manner in which the figure of the eschatological prophet is understood in the New Testament is beyond the scope of this monograph.[22]

The developments in prophetic traditions during the sixth century not only spelled the end of classical prophecy in the Israelite community but also established the formative pattern in which prophecy would be viewed in the future: the return of prophecy either in the form of an individual or as the spirit of prophecy given to the entire religious community. Prophecy in the post-exilic period did not develop unilaterally into apocalyptic. Prophetic traditionists preserved earlier collections and added to them without claiming authority for themselves as prophets. On the other hand, the Chronicler recorded attempts of certain cultic functionaries, the Levitical singers, to attain prophetic status. These singers were the group against which the traditionists wrote when condemning prophecy and were the group in spite of which the traditionists looked forward to the return of legitimate prophecy on the day of Yahweh.

[1]Hanson, *The Dawn of Apocalyptic* 274-276.

[2]See J. Miller, "The Korahites of Southern Judah: The Korahite Psalms," *CBQ* 32 (1970) 58-68, who argues on the basis of an Arad ostracon which contains the phrase *"bny qrḥ"* that the Korahite psalms are pilgrimage songs written by Korahites who originally lived in Judah.

[3]Cf. H. Gunkel on the prophetic element in the psalms, a theme which Gunkel identifies by the presence of "eschatology" in certain psalms; *Einleitung in die Psalmen. Die Gattung der religiösen Lyrik Israels* (Göttingen: Vandenhoeck & Ruprecht, 1933) 329-381.

[4]M. Buss, "The Psalms of Asaph and Korah," *JBL* 82 (1963) 383.

[5]*Ibid.* 391.

[6]Notice should be taken of Josephus' claim to have both priestly and prophetic powers. Perhaps the attempts of the Levitical prophets provided the basis for this self-understanding. See J. Blenkinsopp, "Prophecy and Priesthood in Josephus," *JJS* 25 (1974) 239-262.

[7]See Steck's *Israel und das gewaltsame Geschick der Propheten* where he argues that this tradition is more a way of speaking about Israel's apostasy than an historical report on the fate of the prophets.

[8]E. Fascher's *PROPHETES: Eine Sprach- und Religions-geschichtliche Untersuchung* (Giessen: A. Töpelmann, 1927) remains the standard work on prophecy in the Greco-Roman world. Two traditio-historical works on prophecy deserve special mention: O. Steck, *Israel und das gewaltsame Geschick der Propheten* and W. Meeks, *The Prophet-King: Moses Traditions and the Johannine Christology* (Leiden: Brill, 1967). As for prophecy in the Rabbinic literature, there are few adequate studies. See provisionally: J. Bowman, "Prophets and Prophecy in Talmud and Midrash," *EvQ* 22 (1950) 107-114, 205-220, 255-275; N. Glatzer, "A Study of the Talmudic Interpretation of Prophecy," *Rev Rel* 10 (1946) 115-137; P. Krüger, "Die Würdigung der Propheten im Spätjudentum," *Neutestamentliche Studien* (Leipzig: J. Hinrichs'sche Buchhandlung, 1914) 1-12; O. Michel, "Spätjüdisches Prophetentum," *Neutestamentliche Studien für Rudolph Bultmann* (ed. W. Eltester; Berlin: A. Töpelmann, 1954) 60-66; W. Foerster, "Der heilige Geist im Spätjudentum," *NTS* 8 (1961-62) 117-122.

[9]M. Shepherd, "Prophet in the New Testament," *IDB* Vol 3, 919.

[10]See the appendix, "The Eschatological Prophet," in F. Hahn, *The Titles of Jesus in Christology. Their History in Early Christianity* (London: Lutterworth, 1969) 352-406, for an excellent introduction and bibliography on this topic. Cf. also H. Teeple, *The Mosaic Eschatological Prophet* (Philadelphia: SBL, 1957).

[11]Other important apocryphal and pseudepigraphical texts dealing with the end of prophecy and the expectation of its return include: 1 Mac 9:27, 54; 14:41; Sir 24:33; 49:6-10; Wis 7:22-27; 1 Enoch 108:6; T Levi 8:13-19; T Benj 3:8; 9:2; Sib Or 3:670-829; As Mos 1:5; 2 Apoc Bar 85:3-4.

[12]On prophecy in the Qumran texts, see M. Burrows, "Prophecy and Prophets at Qumran," *Israel's Prophetic Heritage*, 223-232; J. Giblet, "Prophetisme et attente d'un Messie prophète dans l'ancien Judaisme," *L'attente du Messie* (Paris: Desclee de Brouwer, 1954) 85-130; W. Meeks, *The Prophet-King*, 168-171; R. Schnackenburg, "Die Erwartung des 'Propheten' nach dem Neuen Testament und den Qumran Texten," *Studia Evangelica* (Berlin: Akademie Verlag, 1959) 622-639; W. Foerster, "Der heilige Geist im Spätjudentum," 122-134.

[13]R. Brown, "The Messianism of Qumran," *CBQ* 19 (1957) 61. Furthermore, in light of the close relationship between prophet and king in classical Israelite prophecy, I find it most interesting that this relationship is projected into future expectations that the prophet will precede the royal Messiah, cf. Mark 9:11-13.

[14]J. Starcky, "Un texte messianique araméen de la grotte 4 de Qumran," *Ecole des Langues orientales anciennes de l'Institue Catholique de Paris: Mémorial du cinquantenaire* (Paris: Bloud et Gay, 1964) 51-66. Cf. F. Hahn who contends the Qumran community focused only on the Moses typology for the eschatological prophet, *The Titles of Jesus in Christology*, 362.

[15]Vermes, *The Dead Sea Scrolls*, 50.

[16]See Meeks, *The Prophet-King*, 169-171, for a summary of the argument.

[17]Vermes, *The Dead Sea Scrolls*, 236.

[18]Brown, "The Messianism of Qumran," 73ff.

[19]On prophecy in the New Testament, see provisionally, H. A. Guy, *New Testament Prophecy* (London: Epworth, 1947).

[20]It is interesting that in Justin's "Dialogue with Trypho" Elijah is also depicted as the forerunner of the royal Messiah, A. R. Higgins, "Jewish Messianic Belief in Justin Martyr's 'Dialogue with Trypho'," *Nov Test* 9 (1967) 298ff.

[21]For example, Matt 13:57; 21:11, 46; 23:37; Luke 4:24; 7:16; 13:33-34; 24:19; Mark 6:4; John 1:21-25; 4:19-44; 7:40; 9:17. See also provisionally, P. E. Davies, "Jesus and the Role of the Prophet," *JBL* 64 (1945) 214-254; F. W. Young, "Jesus the Prophet: A Reexamination," *JBL* 68 (1949) 285-299.

[22]For discussion of the merging prophetic and royal traditions, see F. Hahn, *The Titles of Jesus and Christology,* and W. Meeks, *The Prophet-King.*